THE UPPER ROOM

WHERE THE WORLD MEETS TO PRAY

Daniele Och
UK editor

INVITATIONAL
INTERDENOMINATIONAL
INTERNATIONAL

37 LANGUAGES
Multiple formats are available in some languages

15 The Chambers, Vineyard
Abingdon OX14 3FE
brf.org.uk

Bible Reading Fellowship is a charity (233280)
and company limited by guarantee (301324),
registered in England and Wales

ISBN 978 1 80039 138 3

Originally published in the USA by The Upper Room® **upperroom.org**

Acknowledgements
Scripture quotations marked with the following abbreviations are taken from the
version shown. Where no acronym is given, the quotation is taken from the same
version as the headline reference.

MSG: The Message copyright © 1993, 1994, 1995, 1996, 2000, 2001, 2002 by Eugene
H. Peterson. Used by permission of NavPress. All rights reserved. Represented by
Tyndale House Publishers, Inc.

NIV: The Holy Bible, New International Version (Anglicised edition) copyright © 1979,
1984, 2011 by Biblica. Used by permission of Hodder & Stoughton Publishers, an
Hachette UK company. All rights reserved. 'NIV' is a registered trademark of Biblica.
UK trademark number 1448790.

NRSV: The New Revised Standard Version of the Bible, Anglicised Edition, copyright
© 1989, 1995 by the Division of Christian Education of the National Council of the
Churches of Christ in the USA. Used by permission. All rights reserved.

CEB: copyright © 2011 by Common English Bible.

KJV: the Authorised Version of the Bible (The King James Bible), the rights in which
are vested in the Crown, are reproduced by permission of the Crown's Patentee,
Cambridge University Press.

ESV: The Holy Bible, English Standard Version, published by HarperCollins
Publishers, © 2001 Crossway Bibles, a division of Good News Publishers. Used by
permission. All rights reserved.

A catalogue record for this book is available from the British Library

Printed by Gutenberg Press, Tarxien, Malta

How to use *The Upper Room*

The Upper Room is ideal in helping us spend a quiet time with God each day. Each daily entry is based on a passage of scripture and is followed by a meditation and prayer. Each person who contributes a meditation to the magazine seeks to relate their experience of God in a way that will help those who use *The Upper Room* every day.

Here are some guidelines to help you make best use of *The Upper Room*:

1 Read the passage of scripture. It is a good idea to read it more than once, in order to have a fuller understanding of what it is about and what you can learn from it.
2 Read the meditation. How does it relate to your own experience? Can you identify with what the writer has outlined from their own experience or understanding?
3 Pray the written prayer. Think about how you can use it to relate to people you know or situations that need your prayers today.
4 Think about the contributor who has written the meditation. Some users of the *The Upper Room* include this person in their prayers for the day.
5 Meditate on the 'Thought for the day' and the 'Prayer focus', perhaps using them again as the focus for prayer or direction for action.

Why is it important to have a daily quiet time? Many people will agree that it is the best way of keeping in touch every day with the God who sustains us and who sends us out to do his will and show his love to the people we encounter each day. Meeting with God in this way reassures us of his presence with us, helps us to discern his will for us and makes us part of his worldwide family of Christian people through our prayers.

I hope that you will be encouraged as you use the magazine regularly as part of your daily devotions, and that God will richly bless you as you read his word and seek to learn more about him.

Daniele Och
UK editor

Could you write a meditation for *The Upper Room*?

The Upper Room is, as far as we know, unique in that its readers are its writers. Known as the place 'where the world meets to pray', contributors from the widest imaginable range of backgrounds and locations share their faith experiences and biblical insights with the entire *Upper Room* community.

BRF publishes the UK edition of *The Upper Room*, and editor Daniele Och is on the lookout for some new UK-based writers. If you think you could write a short meditation on a Bible verse, rooted in your own experience, why not have a go? Each day's meditation aims to help people make a connection between their lives and what God is doing in the world, but to have any chance of being published, it's important to write in an appropriate style. You need to include:

1 a Bible reading and quotation
2 the meditation (200–250 words)
3 a short prayer
4 a Thought for the day
5 a Prayer focus

The maximum word count for all these elements together is 300. Send your reflection by email to **theupperroom@brf.org.uk**. Alternatively, submissions can be sent by post to **The Upper Room, BRF, 15 The Chambers, Vineyard, Abingdon, Oxford OX14 3FE** but please include an email address or phone number. Make sure your name and contact details are clear. Only successful contributors will be contacted and no correspondence will be entered into. A modest fee is paid for successful submissions.

Top tips for writing for *The Upper Room*

- Begin by studying and meditating on the Bible, so that its power supports your words.
- Connect scripture with your own life. Your experience is unique.
- Make only one point.
- Avoid using very familiar illustrations – try to be original.
- Avoid the use of 'You should...', 'You need to...', 'You must...'
- Use language and examples that appeal to the senses.
- Indicate which Bible version you use for quotations.
- Remember your audience.

Good luck! We look forward to reading your meditation.

Waypoint

Stephen replied… 'The God of glory appeared to our ancestor Abraham when he was in Mesopotamia, before he lived in Haran, and said to him, "Leave your country and your relatives and go to the land that I will show you." Then he left the country of the Chaldeans and settled in Haran. After his father died, God had him move from there to this country in which you are now living.'
Acts 7:1–4 (NRSV)

In the passage above, Stephen opens his prophetic sermon with the sojourn of Abraham. Because we know the end of Abraham's story, it is easy to gloss over the fact that Abraham almost didn't make it to the promised land. As Stephen states, Abraham 'settled' in Haran, about halfway between Ur (modern-day Iraq) and Israel. According to Genesis 12, it took a renewed and direct call from God to move Abraham from his comfort zone.

As we enter the midpoint of the calendar year, this is a good opportunity to evaluate our own comfort zones. Are there ways in which we have stopped short of fulfilling God's gospel call? Have we settled for a waypoint rather than fully making room for the reign of God to flourish?

Jesus asks those who follow him to risk living beyond the borders of comfort and familiarity – the settled – and to follow him into whatever and among whoever may lie ahead; for, as Jesus said, 'No procrastination. No backward looks. You can't put God's kingdom off till tomorrow. Seize the day' (Luke 9:62, MSG).

Revd Kimberly Orr
World editor and publisher

Norwegian edition

**Writers featured in this issue
of *The Upper Room*:**
• Kate Carroll (Ireland)
• Øystein Brinch (Norway)

Gifts to the international
editions of *The Upper Room*
help the world meet to pray.
upperroom.org/gift

The editor writes...

I lift up my eyes to the hills. From where does my help come? My help comes from the Lord, who made heaven and earth.
Psalm 121:1–2 (NIV)

Towards the end of last year, as I was editing this issue, I spent several evenings helping out as a stagehand for a local amateur production of *The Sound of Music*. It was the first time I had been part of a theatre crew, and it was exciting to see all the activity that takes place out of sight of the audience.

'Out of sight' was very much our mantra as stagehands. We had to wear dark clothing, preferably black, and try to carry out the scene changes quickly but quietly and before the stage lighting came on for the next scene. (I often failed to meet any of those goals.) When setting up the stage at each venue, the stage manager stuck a line of tape to the floor at the sides of the stage. This marked the 'sight line', separating the wings from the stage – that is, the line between being out of and within the audience's line of sight.

Our 'line of sight' is the theme of many meditations in this issue – whether that be where we focus our attention (18 May), gaining a new perspective (29 May), noticing signs of God's presence (27 July) or the ways in which God's care for us often goes unseen (12 August). Indeed, in one reflection, the author draws lessons from all the work that goes on 'Behind the scenes' at the theatre (see 15 June), something I now have a greater appreciation for.

In the final scene of *The Sound of Music*, as the Trapp family are anxious about fleeing across the mountains into Switzerland on foot, the Mother Abbess quotes Psalm 121:1, encouraging them to change their 'line of sight' – to see the mountains not as a barrier, but as the means by which God would bring their salvation. I pray that the meditations in this issue will likewise encourage us, in whatever circumstances we find ourselves, to change our perspective: to fix our eyes on Jesus, the one through whom God has brought our salvation.

Daniele Och
UK editor

A tiny puddle

Read 2 Corinthians 3:12–18

All of us are looking with unveiled faces at the glory of the Lord as if we were looking in a mirror. We are being transformed into that same image from one degree of glory to the next degree of glory. This comes from the Lord, who is the Spirit.
2 Corinthians 3:18 (CEB)

On my way to work in the morning, I looked up at the sky. The rain during the night had stopped and I could see blue sky between the parting clouds. The edges of the clouds were shining in the morning sun. I was moved by the great beauty of nature that God has created, and I slowed down to gaze at the sky.

Then I noticed a small puddle on the ground. It was surrounded by pebbles and mud. However, a portion of the beautiful sky above was reflected in its tranquil surface. Then I thought, 'The beautiful sky is like God, and we humans are like the puddle!'

In contrast to the huge sky, the puddle was tiny. Yet its tranquil surface reflected and showed me the beauty of the sky. What about me? Is my heart tranquil and peaceful? Not always. My heart is troubled from time to time.

On Sundays, I go to church and feel peaceful. But when I am back in everyday life, I sometimes find myself getting irritated. I want to be like the tranquil puddle – tiny but peaceful, reflecting God's love and sharing it with others.

Prayer: *Dear God, thank you for offering your great love to us. Calm our souls, and use us to reflect your love. Amen*

Thought for the day: When my heart is at peace, I can reflect God's great love.

Hisako Adachi (Kanagawa, Japan)

PRAYER FOCUS: THOSE WHO TRAVEL TO WORK

No distance in prayer

Read Matthew 8:5–13

'Where two or three are gathered in my name, I am there among them.'
Matthew 18:20 (NRSV)

When I served as a pastor at a church in Pennsylvania, someone called me with a personal concern. As the conversation ended, I asked if I could pray with him. Sounding surprised, he asked, 'Can we do that over the phone?' Praying over the phone was new for him. Maybe it doesn't sound strange to us today, but it's easy to resist at first that which is different. But we prayed, and God did the rest.

Every generation creates new ways of expressing love for Christ. As a pastor, I am always searching for innovative ways to reach people. Social media has become the new way to proclaim the same message: Jesus and his redeeming love for us on the cross.

We hear this word from Matthew's gospel: 'Where two or three are gathered in my name, I am there among them.' Christ is the glue that binds us even through our new technologies. Years ago, I heard another phrase that stuck with me, and I think about it when I pray with people over the phone or on social media: 'There is no distance in prayer.' Because of Christ, we have a strong connection holding us together!

Prayer: *Dear Lord, remind us that you can draw us together in community no matter the physical distance between us. In your holy name we pray. Amen*

Thought for the day: There is no distance in prayer.

Cletus L. Hull III (Pennsylvania, USA)

Spiritual clutter

Read Jeremiah 4:14–18

O Jerusalem, wash your heart clean of wickedness so that you may be saved. How long shall your evil schemes lodge within you?
Jeremiah 4:14 (NRSV)

The apartment building I had lived in for four years closed. As my neighbours and I began to move out, I marvelled at the amount of stuff people had been able to fit into their apartments. My own quarters had been pretty bare, but there was always plenty of room for the regular stream of friends coming in and out to visit. Had I accumulated more things, there would not have been enough space for all of the shared meals, impromptu dancing and games of charades with those I cared about.

Though I'm not an avid collector of material possessions, I do have a tendency to store up unnecessary and even dangerous things in my heart: grudges, harsh words, hypocritical thoughts and bad attitudes. My heart can become so disorderly that there's little room left for God or other people. Unless I give the Holy Spirit complete freedom to remove everything that isn't valuable, I will remain isolated in the cramped confines of spiritual clutter.

God longs to live close to us, to share the space of our lives so we can enjoy intimacy with God and with one another. Clearing the junk out of our hearts can be difficult, but when we do, we open ourselves to experiencing life as God meant it to be.

Prayer: *Dear God, thank you for loving us enough to enter our messy hearts and clear space for eternal life. Amen*

Thought for the day: What do I need to clean out of my heart to make more room for God?

Megan L. Anderson (Indiana, USA)

Standing strong

Read Daniel 1:1–15

If sinners entice you, do not consent.
Proverbs 1:10 (NRSV)

Sitting in a hall with my fellow university classmates, we waited in tense silence for the French test to be distributed. This was my final language exam, and I needed to pass. But when the test was handed out, I couldn't make sense of it. I noticed my classmates cheating and was tempted to join them, thinking, 'Cheat now and repent later. God is merciful, right? You don't want to risk failing.'

We've all experienced situations like this. Like Eve, we feel tempted by fruit that would compromise the life God wants us to have. The key to standing our ground against temptation is to know our convictions and commit to them in our hearts.

Daniel modelled this when he resolved to keep the diet laid out in the Jewish law and avoid foods provided by the king of Babylon. God honoured and rewarded his commitment. When we know what our faith requires and commit to it, we can fight temptation – even if that means failing and retaking a French test, like I did.

Prayer: *Dear Lord, teach us the truth of your word. Empower us to live in ways that glorify you. Amen*

Thought for the day: I will commit to God's way, knowing that it is always better.

Joseph Adeoye (Kwara, Nigeria)

Promise of peace

Read 2 Corinthians 9:6–11

*The peace of God, which transcends all understanding, will guard
your hearts and your minds in Christ Jesus.*
Philippians 4:7 (NIV)

Since my husband, Doug, became ill a few years ago, we've curtailed
many of our activities, including driving in the snow. When it snows on a
Sunday, we have a home worship service together. Doug plays the piano,
we take turns reading scripture and we listen to a sermon online.

One Sunday, I couldn't concentrate on our worship. Snow had fallen
fast during the night, and I was worried about clearing the driveway.
'How can I possibly shovel it by myself?', I thought. We were nearly
finished with our service when I heard scraping outside. I peeked out
the window and saw two neighbour boys clearing the driveway. What
an answer to our need! Since then, the boys have shovelled for us whenever it snows.

Philippians 4:6 tells us not to be anxious, but to present our requests
to God with thanksgiving. This command comes with a promise: the
peace of God. I am not sure I prayed about shovelling the snow that
day. But since then, whenever I face a new challenge, I pray, 'Lord, you
know we need… Thank you for your provision.' Answers don't always
come in the way I expect. Sometimes God shows me how I can handle the
task; other times God sends someone to help. No matter the situation,
God provides.

Prayer: *Heavenly Father, help us trust that you will provide what we
need. Banish anxiety from our hearts, and fill us with peace. Amen*

Thought for the day: God knows exactly what I need today.

Elizabeth Erlandson (Nebraska, USA)

Rest for the weary

Read Ephesians 4:17–28
Do not be conformed to this world, but be transformed by the renewing of your minds, so that you may discern what is the will of God – what is good and acceptable and perfect.
Romans 12:2 (NRSV)

Every day I get a peaceful moment when my daughter has gone to sleep for the night and the house is cleaned from the day's activities. This is the moment when my weary soul longs for rest. In the early days of parenthood, I sought this rest on our couch in front of the TV or scrolling through social media on my phone. I learned very quickly that this did not give me the rest I sought so desperately. I became aware that filling my weary soul with entertainment and counsel from the world yielded undesirable results – a quicker temper, shorter patience and selfishness.

It was then that I read Paul's words to the Romans to 'be transformed by the renewing of your minds.' For me, that renewal comes from intentional time spent in God's word and an effort to grow my relationship with Christ. Whether I exchange a TV show for a Christian podcast, or replace time on social media with time spent reading scripture or quiet time in prayer, God is sufficient to sustain me. The things of this world may sparkle and promise rest, but only God can truly renew our weary souls.

Prayer: *Loving God, thank you for the riches of your word and for opportunities to rest. May our lives glorify you. Amen*

Thought for the day: Time spent in God's word gives rest to my weary soul.

Sarah Hopkins (Colorado, USA)

The land of 'What Is'

Read Job 38:1–11

I know the plans I have for you, says the Lord, plans for your welfare and not for harm, to give you a future with hope.
Jeremiah 29:11 (NRSV)

I had told my new roommates that the renovations to our rented apartment would be complete before school started. But there we were, with a week of online school behind us and still no apartment. I felt responsible and blamed myself. What if I had communicated more with our landlord? What if I had found another place as a backup? What if, what if, what if?

It is easy to get caught up in the land of 'What If,' but as I thought over scripture, I remembered the words from Jeremiah quoted above and God's words to Job, 'Who is this that darkens counsel by words without knowledge?' (Job 38:2). Who am I to put my plans above God's? And when I dwell in the land of 'What If,' I put my own plans and abilities before my trust in God. If I truly believe that God has great plans for me, I should stop asking 'What if?' and trust God.

Now, as I sip warm coffee at the breakfast table in my completed apartment, happily moved in with my roommates, I try my best to live in the land of 'What Is' – the place where God lives.

Prayer: *Dear Lord, thank you for the good plans you have for us. Give us the strength to trust you. Amen*

Thought for the day: I will trust God's good plan for my life.

Samuel Wagner (California, USA)

A steady path

Read Luke 18:15–17

Start children off on the way they should go, and even when they are old they will not turn from it.
Proverbs 22:6 (NIV)

My life has been full of strong role models. My mother was head of the household and the single parent of six children. She worked from morning till night to support us. My grandmother Bertha left us a great legacy, teaching us by example to be hardworking and strong, instilling in us the assurance that God is always with us.

In the afternoons, my grandmother would permit us to visit Doña Esther, a woman from the neighbourhood who enjoyed looking after children. She always prepared something delicious to eat. While we ate, she read aloud stories and parables from the Bible. These stories left a deep impression in my young heart and mind, and my life began to change. Despite financial constraints, my constant hope and prayer was to continue my studies. I asked God to help me reach my goal of becoming a teacher.

I persevered, and my goal became a reality. My cornerstone of faith was laid by the strong people in my life who followed the teaching to 'start children off on the way they should go…' Because of their guidance, I remain on a steady path that leads to God.

Prayer: *Dear God, thank you for people of faith who mentor children and provide opportunities for them to know you. Amen*

Thought for the day: How can I encourage someone to seek the path that leads to God?

Gloria Amparo Valencia Riascos (Valle del Cauca, Colombia)

God, where are you?

Read Isaiah 53:1–5

He was wounded for our transgressions, he was bruised for our iniquities: the chastisement of our peace was upon him; and with his stripes we are healed.
Isaiah 53:5 (KJV)

'God, where are you?' I was 22 when I first asked this question. A horrific car crash had left me with a ten per cent chance of survival, yet miraculously I am still here. Now in my 60s, I am finding it easier to see God's work in my life.

I grew up in a Christian household, made a profession of faith at age 12 and have been a Christian since. When I was young, I mistakenly believed that being Christian should give me protection from suffering. But this is simply not true. It was not true for Christ, nor is it true for his followers.

Looking at my life that has included multiple surgeries and physical maladies, an onlooker might mistakenly assume that God was far removed from me. But that would be a mistake. I saw God's hand at work when surgeons changed their minds at the last minute, when treatment plans were altered and when surgery revealed results dramatically different from x-rays. God was present in the support of friends and family who prayed and offered words of encouragement. God was there all along.

Prayer: *Heavenly Father, hear our cry. We pray that you will surround the oppressed, the downtrodden and those sick in body and spirit with your comfort and your love. Amen*

Thought for the day: I will not let my circumstances define my relationship with God.

Dean Gammons (North Carolina, USA)

Tangible acts of love

Read Deuteronomy 15:7–11

The Lord replied, 'My Presence will go with you, and I will give you rest.'
Exodus 33:14 (NIV)

My friend and I had decided to take regular walks through the Siberian village where we were living to pray for our neighbours and to ask for God's guidance in how best to show them love. One brisk fall morning, we prayed for opportunities to be God's hands and feet to our neighbours.

The very next day, God began to answer our prayer, and neighbours began to ask us for help. This had never happened before! An elderly neighbour needed gas for his stove. Another neighbour's well was broken, and she was home with her three young kids. We were easily able to get water for her. One neighbour was in the hospital and needed diapers for her baby. Another family's car broke down, so I offered to drive them in my car.

Such situations continue to this day. People are grateful and amazed that we help them so readily, and they are more open to hearing about Jesus when they experience these tangible acts of love. I am thankful for the way God has answered our prayers so that we are able to shine God's light. Serving others has been a joy rather than a burden because of God's perfect presence and provision.

Prayer: *Dear Lord, help us to be your hands and feet to the world around us. Amen*

Thought for the day: If I ask, God will give me opportunities to show love to others.

Jami Gustafson (Buryatiya, Russia)

Share my joy

Read Luke 15:8–10

Rejoice with those who rejoice, weep with those who weep.
Romans 12:15 (NRSV)

The woman in Jesus' parable was so happy to find her lost coin that she had to tell her neighbours. I felt like I could relate to her joy. After I won custody of my children, I moved to a new town to start a new job doing what I loved. I wanted to celebrate my joy at this new beginning.

As I began looking for a church home in my new town, however, every sermon I heard was about how Christ comforts us in our troubles and the church is there for us in our sorrows. I knew that, but I also wanted to hear the message that the church cared about my happiness. It was frustrating to want to share joy when all I encountered was sympathy. When one pastor happened to mention that God cares about our joy as well as our sorrows, I returned to that church.

There had been sad times before in my life and there have been others since then, but at that time, I needed to know that God and the church were rejoicing with me. I have resolved to be more sensitive to what is going on in others' lives so that if someone is sad, I can empathise, and if someone is happy, I can rejoice with them. When we pay attention to others' feelings, we can build a community that is present and supportive in all circumstances. We all need to know we are not alone, no matter what.

Prayer: *Dear Lord, you have created us for each other. Help us to rejoice with those who are happy just as we weep with those who are sad. Amen*

Thought for the day: How can I share in someone's joy today?

Thomas Blanton (North Carolina, USA)

I am here, not there

Read Isaiah 43:16–21

'Forget the former things; do not dwell on the past.'
Isaiah 43:18 (NIV)

While straightening up a few bottles and jars on my bathroom counter one morning, I found myself lost in a memory of a bathroom in an apartment I had rented when I was young. It wasn't a happy memory, and my mood started sinking. But then I said to myself, 'I'm not there, thank God.' And the memory evaporated, to my great relief.

For a long time, I fought a losing battle with bad memories. They entered my mind like a train I couldn't stop. Once they were there, I was caught up in a vortex, wrestling disturbing emotions, overanalysing and futilely trying to redo events.

But lately the Lord has been showing me simple ways to give these intrusions to God. Just saying something like, 'Thank you, Jesus, that I'm here and not there,' or, 'Praise you that my life is so much better now, God,' stops the memory and brings me back to the present.

After so many years of struggle, I'm amazed and delighted to be able to replace the bad memories of the past with God's refreshing love and blessings in my life today. I am reminded that the Lord has set me free (see John 8:36).

Prayer: *Dear God, thank you for helping us bear our burdens and for breathing new hope into us. Amen*

Thought for the day: With God I can move beyond the negative memories that limit my life.

Victoria Walsh (Montana, USA)

Being Jesus' disciples

Read Luke 10:1–12

'Go on your way. See, I am sending you out like lambs into the midst of wolves.'
Luke 10:3 (NRSV)

The memory of three churches in Surabaya being bombed in the middle of Sunday services in 2018 is still clear in my mind. It was a devastating moment, especially for Christians in Indonesia. Many people were injured or killed, and we hope that such an event will never happen again.

Being a Christian is not always easy. Even Jesus said in the scripture that he sends us like lambs into the midst of wolves. It can be a dangerous task to follow Christ. Nevertheless, Jesus told us that he will be with us as we keep the faith and follow him.

Jesus also told us to love our enemies. Even when people hate, suppress or persecute us, we should never hold grudges. In fact, we should seek others' well-being, pray to God on their behalf and help them. For we are all the children of our Father in heaven, and Christ's love lives in us through the Holy Spirit.

Prayer: *Heavenly Father, give us the strength and courage to follow Christ, to share the good news and to love our enemies. We pray the prayer Jesus taught us, 'Our Father which art in heaven, Hallowed be thy name. Thy kingdom come. Thy will be done, as in heaven, so in earth. Give us day by day our daily bread. And forgive us our sins; for we also forgive every one that is indebted to us. And lead us not into temptation; but deliver us from evil.'* Amen*

Thought for the day: Following Christ is not easy, but the Spirit always accompanies us.

Matheus Claus (Jakarta, Indonesia)

Living by faith

Read Psalm 116:1–9

Return, O my soul, to your rest, for the Lord has dealt bountifully with you.
Psalm 116:7 (NRSV)

Two years ago, my life appeared to be in perfect order. My relationship, finances, education and career all seemed to be succeeding. Around that time, I copied down Psalm 116:7 and hung it in my kitchen. When I looked at that verse, I felt inspired to give thanks. It was easy to give thanks when I didn't have any major problems, but I also asked God to increase my faith so that I could be grateful even if circumstances changed.

I believe the Holy Spirit inspired those prayers for faithfulness because my apparent success evaporated. I lost my job. My hopes for a relationship fell through, and I found myself grieving and feeling forgotten. Everyone around me seemed to be achieving their dreams while I had taken several giant steps back. But every time I looked at Psalm 116:7 hanging in my kitchen, I recalled God's faithfulness.

I suspect no one would look at my circumstances today and claim that I have it all together. But as I continue to grow in this new season, I can still declare that God is bountiful and faithful because God prepared me for this journey. I am learning to live by faith rather than sight.

Prayer: *Dear Lord, help us to love and trust you no matter what happens in our lives. Help us to stay faithful to you, as you are faithful to us. Amen*

Thought for the day: God is faithful no matter what challenges I face.

Rachael Pittiglio (Michigan, USA)

Preparing the way

Read Matthew 3:1–12

A voice of one calling: 'In the wilderness prepare the way for the Lord; make straight in the desert a highway for our God.'
Isaiah 40:3 (NIV)

I like to hike, so I volunteered to help clear a new path at a local nature area. Walking to our work area wasn't easy. We crossed a couple of streams, inched down steep inclines and trudged up hills. Carrying sharp tools made the journey even more difficult. Thankfully, our project leader had prepared for our arrival by tying ropes to sturdy trees that enabled us to descend and climb slippery slopes.

After several hours of cutting back limbs and removing small saplings, we reached the top of a hill and were rewarded with a beautiful view of the lake. Because of our work, future hikers will enjoy the same view, then continue on down the completed trail.

As I worked, the words, 'Prepare the way for the Lord,' came to mind. I thought about how John the Baptist prepared the way for Jesus' ministry and how Jesus prepared the disciples to spread the gospel. Each generation of Christians paves the way for the next. Scripture, prayer and the support of fellow Christians guide us on our spiritual journey. With these tools, we are well prepared to tell people we meet about Jesus.

Prayer: *Heavenly Father, thank you for the faithful Christians who have spread the gospel through the years. Guide us as we prepare the way for new believers. Amen*

Thought for the day: How will I prepare to share Christ with others today?

Kathy Bunse (Missouri, USA)

Holy comforter

Read John 14:23–27

It is expedient for you that I go away: for if I go not away,
the Comforter will not come unto you; but if I depart, I will send him
unto you.
John 16:7 (KJV)

In the last moments Jesus spent with his disciples, he warned them about the persecutions ahead of them if they were to follow him. Jesus did not share this warning to discourage and frighten them but to build their faith and help them understand the journey ahead.

Understanding our challenges can enable us to overcome them. I am proud to be able to testify to this truth. I have encountered many challenges in my life; but the only times I have been able to overcome them were when I understood the root of the problem and trusted in the Lord to help me through.

Knowing that it was not going to be an easy journey, Jesus assured the disciples that they would not be left alone; the Holy Spirit would be their comforter during difficult times, providing peace and consolation in the midst of struggle. This is the work of the Holy Spirit in our lives – to lessen our worry and to calm our fear.

I believe that God wants us to know we are not alone – we have the Holy Spirit to comfort, teach and renew our trust in God. We can trust God and watch for the Holy Spirit's work in our lives.

Prayer: *Dear God, we are grateful for the Holy Spirit, who helps us in the challenges we face. Thank you for the peace only your Comforter can give. Amen*

Thought for the day: In times of fear, I will turn to the Holy Spirit for comfort.

Mark Eshun (Central Region, Ghana)

Chosen people

Read 1 John 3:1–3

You are a chosen people, a royal priesthood, a holy nation, God's special possession, that you may declare the praises of him who called you out of darkness into his wonderful light.
1 Peter 2:9 (NIV)

My three-year-old son, Henrik, was clearly upset as he walked towards me in the church hallway. When I asked him what was wrong, he replied, 'Someone called me a sweetie pie, but I'm *not* a pie! I'm Henrik!' I tried to hide the smile on my face so that he wouldn't think I was laughing at him, then I did my best to explain to him what a 'term of endearment' was.

Henrik loved his name and didn't want anyone to call him anything but that. I walked away thinking about how often we forget what our 'names' are. As we go throughout our day, words get tacked on to us – unloved, dumb, not enough, not attractive, weak, loser. Such labels can cause us to forget who God says we are.

God says we are chosen, loved, pure, free, worthy, strong, victorious, purposed, valuable. Those are just a few of the words our heavenly Father speaks over us. First Peter 2:9 says, 'You are a chosen people, a royal priesthood, a holy nation, God's special possession.' Like Henrik did, remember who you are in Christ and boldly declare truth over yourself today!

Prayer: *Heavenly Father, help us to ignore what others call us. Teach us to declare your truths, believing what your word says about who we are in Christ. Amen*

Thought for the day: Today I will walk confidently because of who I am in Christ.

Rhae Ann Ongstad (Florida, USA)

Resetting my focus

Read 1 Samuel 16:1–13

The heavens declare the glory of God; the skies proclaim the work of his hands.
Psalm 19:1 (NIV)

Today's sky is such a pale gray-blue that it seems as if nothingness curtains the world. On a beautiful Canadian summer day, the sky may be deep blue and either cloudless or contrasted by dazzling white clouds. Vivid shades of orange, red and purple announce sunrise and sunset. Early spring sunshine seems brave, shining with promise. Longing to capture God's marvellous artistry, I take pictures of the sky on the days it intrigues me. But when I look at the pictures later, I am dismayed. The colours are there, but unsightly power lines are prevalent, detracting from the beauty I originally saw. I realise now that I saw only the beauty because I was focused on seeing it.

When I choose to focus on what God has done, I simply enjoy God's sky paintings. The wires are still there, but I don't have to let them diminish my appreciation for God's gift of beauty. I'll keep some of these less-than-ideal pictures to remind me of how to look at others. Do the flaws I notice distract me from the beauty with which God has created each person? I want to see people the way God does!

Prayer: *Forgive us, God, for failing to see beauty in people created in your image. Help us to recognise your delight in them. Amen*

Thought for the day: God's beauty surrounds me. I only need to stop and notice it.

Pat Gerbrandt (Manitoba, Canada)

God's direction

Read Exodus 13:17–22

Whether you turn to the right or to the left, your ears will hear a voice behind you, saying, 'This is the way; walk in it.'
Isaiah 30:21 (NIV)

On a recent flight to visit family, I happened to get a window seat. After we had been in the air a while, I took a break from reading and gazed out the window. The sky was clear blue, and I could see all the way to the ground. We were over sections of land that had no signs of life in any direction. However, I noticed rivers and streams that flowed between the stretches of land. It struck me that the rivers were all winding – not one river ran straight.

I began to think of my life and how it has not run a straight path to where I am today. In today's reading, we see that God did not take Moses and the Israelites on the shortest route to the promised land. Instead, God led them on a long and challenging journey through the desert so that they could avoid war with the Philistines.

Like a winding river, our lives are filled with circuitous changes of direction. But the good news is that just as the river continues to flow, God's directions will take us where God wants us to be. We have only to trust God on the way.

Prayer: *O Lord, thank you for your grace-filled wisdom and guidance. Help us to rely on your directions for our lives and to draw closer to you as we travel the path you intend for us. In Jesus' name, we pray. Amen*

Thought for the day: Regardless of the route, I will embrace God's journey for me.

Brian Foster (North Carolina, USA)

A neighbourly surprise

Read Matthew 22:34–40

Wanting to justify himself, [a lawyer] asked Jesus, 'And who is my neighbour?'
Luke 10:29 (NRSV)

Rain was pouring down, and water and mud from a neighbouring farm were cascading down my hillside and pooling in my backyard. I didn't know these neighbours, and I wondered if they would address the flooding problem or if I would have to find my own solution. I spent a sleepless night going over every scenario, although scripture and God's voice reminded me that I need not worry.

Early the next morning it was still pouring rain, but my neighbours sent me a message saying they had seen the flooding issue and would bring a landscaping professional to assess the situation. They also promised to repair any damage. My worries dissolved. I saw God's Spirit at work and my prayers answered. Where I had expected conflict, God had paved the way for cooperation. These neighbours and I have now formed a wonderful friendship that enriches our lives.

I wonder what opportunities I have missed because of a harsh word in a tense moment. I'm grateful for the example my friends set by responding to a problem in a God-honouring way. I hope I will also be that kind of good neighbour. In our strife-riddled world, may we all be instruments of God's peace.

Prayer: *Heavenly Father, help us remember that we represent you. Let your Spirit guide us so that you can work through us in amazing ways. In Jesus' name. Amen*

Thought for the day: Where can I be a good neighbour and sow seeds of peace?

Suzanne Renfro (Tennessee, USA)

A clear reminder

Read Psalm 91:9–16

God says, 'Because you are devoted to me, I'll rescue you. I'll protect you because you know my name.'
Psalm 91:14 (CEB)

I was driving alone on the highway, still two hours from my destination, when I experienced an overwhelming sense of helplessness so powerful that I decided to pull over. I raised my hands and cried out to God. I wish I could say that crying out to God changed the helplessness I was experiencing, but that was not the case.

However, something else happened that day. I got back on the road, and after driving a few miles, a glorious rainbow came into view. In that moment, my heart filled with hope. That rainbow reminded me of God's faithfulness and reassured me that God remains steadfast, celebrating our joys and embracing us in our struggles.

Burdened with worries and doubts, we sometimes ignore or overlook what God has done in our lives. But that rainbow was a reminder to me that 'Jesus Christ is the same yesterday, today and forever' (Hebrews 13:8). When we cry out to God, we know we can lean on God's promises of mercy and protection: 'I'll be with you in troubling times… I'll show you my salvation' (Psalm 91:15–16).

Prayer: *Our Maker and Protector, thank you for your promises in scripture that are manifested in your care for us. May we always be alert to reminders of your love. Amen*

Thought for the day: I can trust God's promises.

Águeda Suárez (Dominican Republic)

Words of life

Read Romans 8:1–4

If you love me, you will keep my commandments.
John 14:15 (NRSV)

I was not excited to hear that the Ten Commandments were to be our topic of study for the next few weeks. I thought, 'Surely, as we are now in the New Testament era, all these laws are behind us?'

Then I recalled reading about a man who became a Christian while in prison. When he was released, he went into a church for the first time in his life. On the wall, in large letters, were listed the Ten Commandments. His heart sank. He had thought he had been set free, but now, how could he keep all those 'Thou shalt nots'? He brought his despair in prayer to Jesus, and when he looked again, they seemed to read differently. Instead of 'Thou shalt not...', he read them as 'You won't...'

If we come to Jesus as Lord and Saviour, we too will find that not only are our sins forgiven, but also we are given new life in Christ; not only are we are released from condemnation, but also we are empowered by the Holy Spirit to live a life of love that is the fulfilment of the law (see Romans 13:10).

As week by week we have been studying these ten wonderful commands, we have been seeing them now, in the light of Jesus' salvation, not as a means by which God condemns us, but a pattern of the life God enables us to live. How wonderful is God's love for us!

Prayer: *Lord, please help us to love you with all our hearts and to allow you to love our neighbours through us.*

Thought for the day: Through the Spirit, I have God's laws written on my heart.

Pauline Lewis (Wales, United Kingdom)

PRAYER FOCUS: FORMER INMATES

Eat your vegetables

Read John 14:15–21

Jesus replied, 'Anyone who loves me will obey my teaching. My Father will love them, and we will come to them and make our home with them.'
John 14:23 (NIV)

My daughter does not like to eat vegetables. My constant words of encouragement to her that vegetables are good for her health are usually to no avail. But to my surprise, one night she ate all the vegetables on her plate. When I asked her why, she said that she wanted to please me. As we enjoyed that special dinner together, my daughter and I realised God was teaching us something.

My daughter loves me and wants to please me. I think our relationship with God works like that too. When we love and want to please God, we obey God's commands. And in doing this we also do what is best for us. In the same way that I want my daughter to eat vegetables for her own health and well-being, God wants us to obey for our own growth towards Christlikeness.

Prayer: *Dear God, help us to honour and love you by doing all that you have commanded us to do. As Jesus taught us, we pray, 'Our Father in heaven, hallowed be your name, your kingdom come, your will be done, on earth as it is in heaven. Give us today our daily bread. And forgive us our debts, as we also have forgiven our debtors. And lead us not into temptation, but deliver us from the evil one.'* Amen*

Thought for the day: I show my love for God when I follow God's commands.

Lei Cao Garcia-Bote (Kuala Lumpur, Malaysia)

*Matthew 6:9–13

Blessings list

Read Psalm 61:1–8

You, O Lord, are a shield around me, my glory, and the one who lifts up my head.
Psalm 3:3 (NRSV)

My wife and I were both suffering from extended illnesses that had exhausted us physically and financially, with seemingly no end in sight. Struggling constantly to make ends meet, we grew angry and frustrated. But we still read daily the biblical stories of faith, particularly the story of David. He too had suffered much in life, but he never gave up hope in God. We vowed that we wouldn't either.

We made a 'Blessings List' and put it on our refrigerator. On it we wrote down every good thing we had in our lives, no matter how small it might seem. And as we made the list, we began to realise that God had indeed blessed us. We had much to be grateful for, if only we looked at what we had instead of focusing on what we did not have.

We still suffer hardships in our lives; no doubt we always will. But my wife and I keep our blessings list on the refrigerator and update it every day. We have found that in a world with a lot of sickness, gratitude is good medicine.

Prayer: *Our heavenly Father, may we never forget that when so much in life goes wrong, you are always here to redeem our lives and make us truly whole. Amen*

Thought for the day: A grateful attitude helps me remember God's blessings.

Mark A. Carter (Oregon, USA)

Held in prayer

Read Exodus 17:10–13

Aaron and Hur held [Moses'] hands up – one on one side, one on the other – so that his hands remained steady till sunset.
Exodus 17:12 (NIV)

My father taught me the value of self-sufficiency: 'The best job is one you do yourself.' He rarely hired a contractor or asked for help in all the work he did around his home. I took this teaching into other areas of my life, including dealing with stress and grief. I didn't need anyone. I could do everything myself.

When my mother was near death, I held on to this concept by dealing with the caregiving and grief alone. However, I did ask my church group for prayer. As time passed and my mum continued to decline, I found that asking for prayer was vital to my health and well-being. The group's prayers held me aloft, not physically in the way Aaron and Hur supported Moses, but spiritually. When they called to the Lord on my behalf, I felt supported. After my mother died, many in my prayer group came to the service, sent cards and offered hugs. In addition, they held me in prayer for months to come.

I thought I could handle even the most difficult grief by myself, but those prayers held me up, offering me strength when I had none of my own.

Prayer: *Dear Lord, thank you for the gift of prayer and friendship. Thank you for reminding us that we cannot – and do not have to – do everything alone. In Jesus' name. Amen*

Thought for the day: It's okay to ask for help.

Sue A. Fairchild (Pennsylvania, USA)

Focused

Read Psalm 37:1–6

Seek first his kingdom and his righteousness, and all these things will be given to you as well.
Matthew 6:33 (NIV)

Even though I live in a 16-story building in the middle of a big city, there are nearby areas with big trees where birds nest and sing, offering a lovely symphony every morning. As the day continues, the crescendo of the city noise makes it difficult to hear the birds singing.

One day, during my morning prayer time, I realised that listening to the birds singing was good practice for listening to God's voice. I decided then to focus on the sweet singing and block out the routine morning noises of the city. 'This,' I thought, 'is how we are invited to seek and focus on God in the midst of daily distractions.' This focus – our full attention centred on God – is what allows us to draw closer to God, unimpeded by obstacles around us.

In an anxiety-filled world, the intentional study of scripture strengthens our connection with God. Remaining focused on God's voice and presence will prompt us to seek first God's kingdom and righteousness and allow us to rest on God's promises.

Prayer: *Creator God, help us to remain focused on your grace, goodness and the sights and sounds of your presence around us as we seek to serve your kingdom on earth. Amen*

Thought for the day: Amid the distractions, I will focus my attention on God.

Juan Carlos Gómez (Bogotá, Colombia)

Grief and worship

Read Job 1:13–22

Job arose, tore his robe, shaved his head, and fell on the ground and worshipped.
Job 1:20 (NRSV)

The entire two-and-a-half years of my son's life have been filled with health problems. We have dealt with a heart that stopped beating, lungs that stopped breathing and a body that stopped growing. We have seen him struggle to crawl, walk and talk. Now, we are in the middle of more evaluations. I can relate to the difficulties Job faced.

However, there is one part of Job's experience that I do not understand. When his property was stolen, servants murdered and children killed, Job grieved and then worshipped. Needless to say, worship is not at the top of my mind when the doctor calls. Heartbreak? Of course. Anger? Usually. Bitterness? Sometimes. Never worship.

But what if it were? When my son inevitably receives his next diagnosis, what if my initial moments of grief could be followed by worship? At some of the worst moments of my life, what if I turned to God? Maybe that could make all the difference, helping to comfort heartbreak, turn anger to peace and transform bitterness into hope.

God never promises an easy life. We all nod along when the pastor says this, but maybe it's time for me to really start accepting it. If I wake up every day and worship God, then maybe, just maybe, the bad days won't feel so bad.

Prayer: *O Lord, help us to worship you today no matter what our days may bring. Help us to take both the good and the bad and turn it over to you. Amen*

Thought for the day: I will find ways to worship God today, even in my struggles.

Lynnette Tortorich (Wisconsin, USA)

Fighting Goliath

Read 1 Samuel 17:24–37

David said moreover, The Lord that delivered me out of the paw of the lion, and out of the paw of the bear, he will deliver me out of the hand of this Philistine. And Saul said unto David, Go, and the Lord be with thee.
1 Samuel 17:37 (KJV)

When David saw Goliath, he felt called to fight for the honour of God and God's people. But King Saul doubted him, and David watched as all of the other Israelites ran away in fear. These things could have discouraged young David or caused him to be afraid. But he fully trusted in the power of the Almighty and refused to let anything deter him from fighting Goliath.

We each have our own Goliath. It could be job loss, poor grades, an unhealthy relationship, a bad boss or a pandemic. These struggles can seem insurmountable. They can cause panic and fear. But we can always have hope because God is with us, and, like David, we can beat Goliath.

When I resigned from my job in 2015, I did not have a plan, and new jobs were hard to find. But I remembered David's example, and I told myself that God would help me too. In time I got a better job.

As the people of God, we can rise above any setback. We are not overcome by our challenges. No matter what we face, we can feel capable with the Almighty on our side.

Prayer: *Almighty God, just as you helped David, help us to rise above the challenges set before us. Amen*

Thought for the day: I will not be intimidated by any situation, because God is on my side.

Joseph Tosin (Lagos, Nigeria)

A new perspective

Read Nehemiah 8:9–12

This is the day the Lord has made; let us rejoice and be glad in it.
Psalm 118:24 (NRSV)

When I retired, I was determined to stay busy. I had ample time, and I viewed it as an opportunity to serve God by giving back to others. But I kept myself too busy. For a few years I was fine running from one activity or meeting to another, but recently I've been plagued with discontentment – even a deep feeling of sadness. I didn't feel joy, and I didn't know why. After all, wasn't I serving God?

Surprisingly my perspective changed during the pandemic, when all of us were forced to slow down or stop. I began to appreciate simple things, like birds singing in the morning and watching the beauty of spring unfold. Most important, I discovered that in all my busyness, I had been neglecting quiet time with God. No wonder I felt such heaviness and sadness!

I'm making some positive changes now. None of us is guaranteed tomorrow, so I'm focusing on activities that bring me joy as I serve others. I guard my meeting time with God every morning, and that helps me rejoice in each day no matter what may come my way.

Prayer: *Heavenly Father, help us always to seek you first. Thank you for the joy we find in you. Amen*

Thought for the day: Today I will seek God first.

Leonora 'Lee' Smith (North Carolina, USA)

The joy of heaven

Read Revelation 21:1–4

Those who go out weeping… will return with songs of joy.
Psalm 126:6 (NIV)

Recently my husband of 47 years died rather unexpectedly. He had suffered with ill health through most of our married life, and as a result of all the medication had struggled with depression. All his life he had longed to really experience the presence of God with him, but the depression masked his feelings.

I was with him when he died, and it was as though a door into heaven opened – such an overpowering joy poured out! I knew at that moment that he was welcomed into heaven and would really know the joy of being with his Saviour. An unexpected side effect was that I felt as if I was walking on air for at least two weeks, so aware was I of the joy of heaven.

Of course, I miss having my husband here with me, and I wonder what God has next for me according to his promise in Jeremiah 29:11: 'I know the plans I have for you'. But while I wait I cannot forget the joy.

Prayer: *Heavenly Father, thank you that you comfort us when we mourn. Amen*

Thought for the day: One day, God will wipe every tear from my eyes.

Hilary Hartley (England, United Kingdom)

Dealing with distraction

Read 1 Peter 5:6–11

The God of all grace, who called you to his eternal glory in Christ, after you have suffered a little while, will himself restore you and make you strong, firm and steadfast.
1 Peter 5:10 (NIV)

The other night at our evening prayer time, Sister Alegría and I were interrupted by a beetle that was attracted to our hand-held light. The inch-long creature kept landing on our necks, arms and legs with an unpleasant tickle. We brushed the beetle away, but it was nearly impossible to concentrate on our scripture readings. The beetle was not a biting insect, so I didn't want to kill it – though I was tempted. I caught it in my hand and released it outside. Finally we could pray in peace.

This experience is a helpful metaphor for dealing with problems that arise in my life. Sin, temptation, worries and even trivial things can distract me from God during worship and prayer, as well as keep me from living a faithful life. When that happens, instead of just ignoring my problems or trying to brush them away, I would do well to face the challenges straight on and turn them over to God. God has the power to resolve them and guide me in what steps I may need to take. The process may be difficult, but it is worthwhile. When we give God not only our praise but also our problems, our faith will be strengthened and we can regain a sense of peace.

Prayer: *All-powerful God, help us to let go of our problems and distractions so we can focus on you and what's really important in life. Amen*

Thought for the day: I can trade my problems for the peace of God.

Sister Confianza del Señor (Colón, Honduras)

A place to retreat

Read Mark 1:29–39

Very early in the morning, while it was still dark, Jesus got up, left the house and went off to a solitary place, where he prayed.
Mark 1:35 (NIV)

Growing up as the oldest of three sisters with a large extended family, there was never a shortage of siblings, cousins or friends coming and going through our home. For the most part, the constant activity was welcome. Yet there were times when I needed to escape the hustle and bustle.

Just behind our house grew a large lilac bush. When I needed an escape, I would crawl under the blossoming branches and sit hidden from the world. As a cool summer breeze blew through the branches, I would close my eyes and breathe in the sweet fragrance of the lilac. The serenity of this place seemed to melt away the worries of the world.

Scripture shows us the importance of taking time to breathe in God's peace, love and hope. In today's quoted verse, 'Jesus got up, left the house and went off to a solitary place, where he prayed.' Just as I used the lilac bush as a child, today I seek to follow Jesus' example and find a time and place to retreat from the hustle and bustle of daily life to breathe in the sweet fragrance of God's peace. Honouring God in this way brings us the peace, love and hope of God.

Prayer: *Father God, thank you for being with us every moment. Help us to remember that you always offer us peace, hope and joy. Amen*

Thought for the day: Today I will pause to accept the peace God offers.

Mendy Creswell Huskey (Tennessee, USA)

God understands

Read John 15:9–17

God so loved the world that he gave his one and only Son, that whoever believes in him shall not perish but have eternal life.
John 3:16 (NIV)

A few months ago, my wife and I were at a restaurant with another couple, and we were able to talk with them about our faith. The wife told us that she did not have a relationship with God, and she did not want to have one because she had experienced the tragic deaths of her father and her brother in a car accident years ago. She did not understand how there could be a God, given the pain she and her mother felt from those losses. In that moment, I only knew to tell her that I could not imagine the pain they felt but that as a father of two children, I could perceive the depth of their loss.

Days later, during my prayer time, I kept asking myself, 'What answer could I give to that woman and her mother about who God is?' I felt God telling me that God is not rigid and indifferent. God endures the pain and death of people much like we do. And I wished I could have explained that truth to the woman. Because to me, God's act of love in sacrificing his son for our sins and the pain of that loss means that God understands and stands with us in our grief. And perhaps the experience of such a painful loss that woman and her mother suffered could help them understand our loving God more deeply.

Prayer: *God of love, help us to understand and remain deeply aware of your love for us so we can share your hope with those who are suffering. In Jesus' name. Amen*

Thought for the day: Even through suffering, I will remember God's love.

Enric Ainsa i Puig (Aragon, Spain)

Grateful hearts

Read 1 Thessalonians 1:1–10

We always give thanks to God for all of you and mention you in our prayers, constantly remembering before our God and Father your work of faith and labour of love and steadfastness of hope in our Lord Jesus Christ.
1 Thessalonians 1:2–3 (NRSV)

Our pastor recently announced that he will be leaving us in a few months to take a position at another church. I was saddened by this news; his departure will be a great loss. His sustaining message of 'we love because God first loved us' has helped our congregation to become more welcoming. While he has only been with us for a few years, we have attracted a significant number of new members, and he makes everyone feel worthy of his time and attention.

Although I have expressed my appreciation to him a number of times, I wish I had done it more. It is easy to take for granted the love people show us and to assume they will always be there for us. It can also be tempting to criticise others rather than to appreciate the good that they do. But scripture teaches us to show our gratitude for others. This could be with a few words, a note or an action.

In the next few months of transition, I intend to show our pastor the appreciation he deserves. I hope to do the same for my family and friends as well as kind strangers I may encounter. Expressing gratitude is a way to lift up ourselves and others, and it pleases God.

Prayer: *Dear God, thank you for the people who love us and show kindness to us. Inspire us to show our gratitude to them that we may encourage them in their good works. Amen*

Thought for the day: My gratitude can bless others and myself.

Carol J. Giesey (Pennsylvania, USA)

A place of rest

Read Matthew 11:28–30

'Come to me, all you that are weary and are carrying heavy burdens, and I will give you rest.'
Matthew 11:28 (NRSV)

There have been many times in my life when I have felt so overwhelmed that I have become very anxious, critical and hopeless. Being a full-time student with a part-time job and volunteering with a local youth ministry can be exhausting, and I don't have much time for myself. I want to do the best I can, so I put a lot of pressure on myself to succeed. But I often doubt if I'm good enough.

One day I was sitting in my room about to go to class, but I couldn't seem to find the strength. Unexpectedly, I felt a nudge from God to pray. I began to tell God what I had been thinking, what I was feeling and why I felt so down and hopeless. A lot of the internal weight and struggle began to lift as God reminded me that I have a place that's secure and safe for me to be honest. In prayer I have a place to run to when I feel down and a firm place to stand when nothing else is working out for me.

We have a God who truly and deeply cares for us. When the busyness of life begins to overwhelm us, we can remember that Jesus doesn't want us to carry that weight alone. We can hand over our burdens to Jesus who will give us the rest we need.

Prayer: *Dear Jesus, help us to give all our heavy burdens to you. Thank you for renewing us when we feel hopeless. Amen*

Thought for the day: I will give my burdens to God, who always offers help.

Nathan Cox (Texas, USA)

Opportunity to bless

Read Acts 2:37–41

Those who accepted his message were baptised, and about three thousand were added to their number that day.
Acts 2:41 (NIV)

'Thank you, Sister. I'm blessed with your sermon,' said my friend. I had been given the opportunity to preach a sermon in our prayer meeting. Although I had prepared, I was still nervous. On the day of the prayer meeting I was unwell, and shortly after delivering the sermon I felt sad. I said to God, 'I'm sorry, Lord. I'm not good at delivering your words.' But hearing my friend's opinion refreshed my soul.

I was reminded of Peter. On the day of Pentecost, Peter talked about Jesus, and his message transformed people's hearts. They were blessed. Many of them were baptised, and about three thousand were added as believers. Even though Peter had not intended to preach that day, God worked through his message, and Peter was a blessing for many people. Like Peter, so was I! Even though only one friend told me that he had been blessed, I was still very encouraged. I thank God for giving me that opportunity and for the many other opportunities God has opened up for me to be a blessing to others.

Prayer: *Dear God, thank you for the opportunity to bless others. Give us the courage to act on those opportunities. Amen*

Thought for the day: I am happiest when I can bless others by sharing God's good news.

Linawati Santoso (East Java, Indonesia)

You can

Read Matthew 14:22–36

For we are God's handiwork, created in Christ Jesus to do good works, which God prepared in advance for us to do.
Ephesians 2:10 (NIV)

My husband and I have two adopted children. They had a rough start in life, and because of this it can be hard for them to leave us to go to school. We recently had six months at home due to Covid-19, so on their return to school, we wondered how we'd manage. As we prepared to come back, we had to work on two things: their trust of us, and their belief in themselves.

As I watched our son bravely walk up the steps to his class, I was willing him on, brimming with pride. Then it was our daughter's turn. 'You can do this,' I said. She steeled herself and, after a couple of false starts, she conquered it, looking back with a little wave.

Jesus was like that for Peter: from the moment they met, Jesus was calling Peter to do more than Peter had ever thought he could do, from being a disciple in the first place, to feeding 5,000, walking on water, healing and eventually speaking to thousands. Peter was learning, again and again, to trust Jesus' voice, saying, 'You can do this.'

Jesus does the same for us. For some of us, it takes faith to just put one foot in front of the other right now. Whatever steps of faith you need to take today, take a moment to hear his voice, telling you 'You can.'

Prayer: *Lord, help me to have faith that with you, I can do this! Amen*

Thought for the day: What is Jesus is calling me to do today?

Amy Turner (England, United Kingdom)

Just a sparrow

Read Luke 12:1–12

'Are not five sparrows sold for two pennies? Yet not one of them is forgotten by God.'
Luke 12:6 (NIV)

My family is fascinated with birds, and we try to identify them whenever we are outside. One morning I saw an unusual and interesting bird. I didn't have binoculars ready, so I tried listening for the bird's song. Unfortunately I couldn't make out its sound because many sparrows were singing at the same time.

I was disappointed as I headed home. I looked up one more time and saw a sparrow flying from roof to roof. I thought, 'It's just a sparrow.' I resented the fact that the sparrows had kept me from identifying the unusual bird. Sparrows are beautiful and sing melodiously, but because I see them all the time they are not exciting to me.

Suddenly, Luke 12:6 came to mind. Even the humble, common sparrow is remembered by God and is under God's sovereign care. Often we feel lonely, forgotten or unimportant. But that doesn't mean we are lost. We can celebrate sparrows, and ourselves, because the Lord knows us and sees us, no matter how humble we may be. And this is the proof: Jesus died for us! Our sovereign God ultimately gives us identity and declares our worth. Just as God does for the sparrows, God always remembers and cares for us.

Prayer: *Sovereign God, we know you look lovingly upon all of your creation. Thank you that all of your creatures are precious in your sight. Amen*

Thought for the day: Even when I feel unimportant, God declares my worth.

Ruthie Solitario (National Capital Region, Philippines)

From grief to hope

Read Psalm 23:1–6

Why are you cast down, O my soul, and why are you disquieted within me? Hope in God; for I shall again praise him, my help and my God.
Psalm 42:11 (NRSV)

One day on a hike, I could see my intended destination: a grove of spruce trees towering above me. However, a thick briar patch stood in my way. Pulling clippers from my back pocket, I grasped the first briar stem, cut it and tossed it aside. Slowly, I cut a trail leading through the thicket of thorns.

Halfway up the hill, I realised how this process paralleled my recent faith journey. For months, grief had overwhelmed me, making daily time with God seem impossible. I knew that scripture answered my sorrow with assurance. But the briars of sadness still seemed to block out hope.

As I pressed on up the hill, I decided to clip my stems of sadness with the 'sword of the Spirit, which is the word of God' (Ephesians 6:17). In rhythm with my snipping of the literal thorns, I repeated Psalm 23. With each cut and phrase, I felt myself step out of the earthly and spiritual valley of briars. Smelling the sweet fragrance of pine, I looked up at the sun-drenched trees swaying as living psalms to their creator. God's creation reminded me that reciting and trusting in God's word sustains us and gives us hope.

Prayer: *Dear Lord, thank you for your word that sustains us in grief. Thank you for meeting us in your creation as a way to comfort, renew and refresh our hearts with hope. Amen*

Thought for the day: God meets me in my sadness.

Karla Sue Lowe-Phelps (Missouri, USA)

Over 150 names

Read James 5:13–16

'I have prayed for you, Simon, that your faith may not fail.'
Luke 22:32 (NIV)

Some years ago after retiring as a pastor, I started to make a list of people to pray for. I couldn't remember the increasing number of names I was concerned about, so I used my computer to record the names – to refresh my memory. I found that new names needed to be added constantly, and that the names of those who had recovered could be removed after a prayer of thanksgiving. Finally, I ended up with an active list of over 150 names, which I still update regularly.

I carry my list with me all the time. When I wake up during the night, I spend time praying for those whose circumstances seem to be a priority. With my list close at hand, I can pray for people at any time of day. And I have found that praying for other people who need God's healing helps to take my mind off my own concerns. Sometimes I tell people, 'You're on my prayer list.' And often they seem strengthened just knowing someone is praying for them.

Who could benefit from your prayers? Remember, Jesus told us, 'I will do whatever you ask in my name, so that the Father may be glorified in the Son' (John 14:13).

Prayer: *Thank you, God, for hearing our prayers. We pray always in the blessed name of your dear Son, Jesus. Amen*

Thought for the day: My spare moments offer opportunities to pray for others.

Gerald H. Ihle (Pennsylvania, USA)

PRAYER FOCUS: RETIRED PASTORS

Limitation or blessing?

Read Acts 10:9–16

'God has shown me that I should not call anyone profane or unclean.'
Acts 10:28 (NRSV)

At 61, with a new degree, I was discouraged. I had not received the job I had applied for with great hope. But then I received a phone call from the monastery where I'd been on a waiting list for a retreat. They had an opening that very weekend.

The day I arrived, the scripture for the afternoon service was the story of Peter's unwillingness to visit Gentiles because he believed they were unclean. I wondered, 'What do I call profane that God blesses?' As I walked the grounds that afternoon, I prayed this question over and over: 'What's holding me back? Lord, what do you bless that I don't?'

As I sat in the chapel once again, God answered my question. It was my fear that I'm too old for a new job, to begin again, that was holding me back from finding my new place of service and a way forward. I felt God encouraging me to move past my prejudice against my age to see new possibilities instead of only limitations. I was seeing age as a problem when God did not!

I left the chapel with this question clearly in my mind: can I look past my biases and see what God blesses in others and in me?

Prayer: *Dear God, help us to face what we falsely see as obstacles that hold us back from your service. Amen*

Thought for the day: What do I call profane that God blesses?

Linda Coggin (British Columbia, Canada)

Beyond measure

Read 2 Kings 6:1–7

*As one was felling a log, his axehead fell into the water; he cried out,
'Alas, master! It was borrowed.'*
2 Kings 6:5 (NRSV)

Sometimes I doubt that God cares about the mundane aspects of my
life. Yet at the same time, how I handle the mundane things reveals my
character. After all, Jesus commends those who are faithful with small
things (see Matthew 25:23).

I work in a research office. A senior professor at the office has a
library of reference books and lets me borrow them. One day the book
I needed was missing. I felt certain I had returned it when I last used it,
but I couldn't be sure. This technical book would be expensive to replace.
Then I remembered Elisha and the floating axe head. I recalled the words
of scripture, 'Alas, master! It was borrowed.' I wanted to demonstrate
godly stewardship and Christian character in the workplace, so I prayed,
'Lord, if I misplaced the book, remind me where I put it. If someone else
took the book, may it be returned.'

After about ten days, the book showed up on the professor's desk.
I don't equate the book's return with a miraculously buoyant axe head,
but I am always encouraged by answered prayer.

God's concern for us is beyond measure. We can trust God to bring
resolution to any situation, even when it seems insignificant.

Prayer: *O Lord, help us to honour you through faithful stewardship of
your gifts. Amen*

Thought for the day: None of my concerns is insignificant to God.

Andrew Michael Ardoin (Louisiana, USA)

Wait for the Lord

Read Psalm 33:16–22

I wait for the Lord, my whole being waits, and in his word I put my hope.
Psalm 130:5 (NIV)

When I became a Christian, my life changed. I developed a deep yearning to know more about Christ and to study God's word. Every day I set aside time for study and reflection. Everything seemed to be going well until my health began to deteriorate. I was in the prime of my life, and I could not understand why this was happening.

After consulting with several doctors and incurring medical bills, my savings began to dwindle. Early one morning on the bus ride to work, I looked out the window and noticed the dry, brown grass along the route. The unforgiving sun and the heat had withered it. I felt the same way – beaten down and sad because of the adversity I now faced. Still, throughout this time, I continued to meditate on God's word and pray for healing.

Several months passed, and then the rains came. I continued to ride the bus to work and watched as the grass along the road became a vibrant green. After a bleak dry season, I saw God's miracle in the healthy new growth of green grass. In the same way, God renews and gives new life and strength to us. God heard my prayers. Even in adversity, God's abiding love and mercy are always present.

Prayer: *Eternal God, help us as we wait and trust in you to learn from the lessons life provides. Amen*

Thought for the day: In any season, I will wait with hope on the Lord.

Ariana Lizbeth Villalobos Yáñez (Morelos, Mexico)

A portrait of Christ

Read 2 Timothy 3:14–17
We are his workmanship, created in Christ Jesus unto good works,
which God hath before ordained that we should walk in them.
Ephesians 2:10 (KJV)

One of my hobbies is painting landscapes. I enjoy looking at God's creation and trying to portray my version of land, sky and water on canvas. In order to paint, I have to study painting techniques and the best way to present natural elements of the earth. It is about mixing colours and using the proper shapes, lighting and perspective. The more I learn about nature, the better I am able to paint because I understand my subject. If I am successful, others can see and understand my paintings and hopefully be inspired by them.

The verse quoted above tells us that God has created us with the potential for doing good works through Jesus Christ. The reading from 2 Timothy talks about the value of Bible study. The more we study, pray and meditate on God's word in the Bible, the better we understand who God is. When God's word becomes part of us through the Holy Spirit, the better we can portray Christ to others when they hear our words and see our actions. When we do this, we become God's witness and exhibit his workmanship. Let us be a portrait of Christ for God's glory throughout the world.

Prayer: *Our Father, help us to know you better through the study of scripture. May your Holy Spirit enable us to be your example in this world so that others will see Christ through us. Amen*

Thought for the day: What can I do to help others see Christ in me?

Verner Guthrie (Alabama, USA)

Do not be afraid

Read Isaiah 43:1–7
This is what the Lord says – he who created you, Jacob, he who formed you, Israel: 'Do not fear, for I have redeemed you; I have summoned you by name; you are mine.'
Isaiah 43:1 (NIV)

God called my husband and me to serve, so we were preparing ourselves for ministry through theological training in Jabalpur. We had our four-year-old son with us, and we were dependent on a stipend we used to receive from the college we were attending. We were facing a financial crisis, but we had faith in God. As we read in Isaiah 43:5, God says, 'Do not be afraid, for I am with you.'

Sometimes I was unsure whether my husband and I would be able to complete our training. Every day we prayed for help because God is the one who called us to prepare for ministry through this training. Those four years of training were a time of crisis and fear, but it was also a time when we received God's love, comfort and peace.

God was with us in every situation, including during sickness, financial crisis and times of need. Now, years later, we are both serving as ordained pastors, and God is also using our son in the work of ministry.

Prayer: *Thank you, Lord, for your love and protection. Be with us as we follow your call. Amen*

Thought for the day: God will help me in every situation.

Saira Verma (Uttar Pradesh, India)

Behind the scenes

Read Romans 16:1–16

Each of you should use whatever gift you have received to serve others, as faithful stewards of God's grace in its various forms.
1 Peter 4:10 (NIV)

I recently viewed an outstanding theatrical performance. At the end of the show the actors returned to the stage one by one and received a standing ovation. Reading through the playbill following the performance, I came across the names of the production crew and was surprised at the large number of individuals working behind the scenes. But unlike the cast, their photos and stories did not appear in the playbill. They were not applauded for their part in the production, but they were crucial to the success of the play.

Most of us are familiar with the names Peter, Paul and Timothy from the Bible, whose contributions to the early church were significant. They were leaders; but they were not alone. In Romans 16, Paul named at least 26 people of diverse backgrounds – men, women, Jews, Gentiles, slaves and prominent citizens – who contributed to the success of the church in various ways. Far from viewing them as unimportant, it is clear that Paul valued them highly. He applauded them for their commitment and hard work. Many of us feel that because we don't serve as leaders, we can't make a difference. Not so. Each of us has gifts that can be useful to serve others and thus glorify God.

Prayer: *O Lord, help us to realise that we are important parts of the body of Christ. Show us ways we can serve others in your name. Amen*

Thought for the day: God values the role I play in the body of Christ.

Wayne Greenawalt (Illinois, USA)

Grace and forgiveness

Read Ephesians 4:1–13

Create in me a pure heart, O God, and renew a steadfast spirit within me.
Psalm 51:10 (NIV)

I recently asked a former co-worker to lunch. It had been years since I last saw him, but I wanted to apologise face-to-face for an incident that happened at the office. In my mind, he had the right to be angry with me, so I arrived at the restaurant ready to face his ill feelings.

To my surprise, he accepted my apology and did not make a big deal about the incident. We spent a pleasant hour together and parted as friends. I left the restaurant with a light heart and a clean conscience.

I used to make decisions based on what would turn out best for me rather than considering others. My selfishness directed my actions. I thought everyone should just take care of themselves. My relationship with Christ has changed my life significantly, and I am no longer the person I was when I mistreated my former co-worker. My creator has forgiven that sin and all of my others. Because of God's grace and forgiveness I can now look back at my life, see my mistakes, and take steps to correct them. In doing so, I have the opportunity to show others what God has done for me. And I am reminded of God's grace when others, such as my friend, accept my apology and offer forgiveness.

Prayer: *Forgiving God, thank you for your grace and mercy. Help us to love others by asking for forgiveness. And give us eyes to see your grace in the lives of those around us. Amen*

Thought for the day: My new life in Christ gives me strength to face my mistakes.

Betsy Mitchell (New York, USA)

Lifeline

Read 2 Corinthians 1:3–7

Encourage one another and build up each other, as indeed you are doing.
1 Thessalonians 5:11 (NRSV)

It was yet another lonely day when the telephone rang. I did not know the person at the other end of the line, but she explained that we belonged to the same church and she had heard of my ill health. She asked if I would appreciate a regular phone call and, perhaps, someone to pray with. I gladly accepted, thanking God for this woman's compassion and faithfulness.

At the time, this woman was busy managing a household with school-aged children as well as operating a small home-based business. But she made a point of calling every few days and asking how I was doing. Even if she only had a few minutes to spare, this regular phone call was a lifeline for me. It reminded me that I had not been forgotten and allowed me to connect with someone.

After 16 years of being virtually housebound, I am still receiving phone calls from this faithful woman of God who has now become a very close friend. And as a result of her act of love and service towards someone she did not know, I have learned the importance of caring for others.

Prayer: *Compassionate God, thank you for the care you show us through the loving actions of others. Help us share your love and encouragement in the same way. In Jesus' name we pray. Amen*

Thought for the day: Whom can I encourage with a phone call today?

Bronwyn Ashton Winch (Queensland, Australia)

Trusting God

Read Matthew 6:25–34

*'Do not worry about tomorrow, for tomorrow will worry about itself.
Each day has enough trouble of its own.'*
Matthew 6:34 (NIV)

I remember watching my dad slowly succumb to Alzheimer's disease. My dad was my hero – my father, my friend, my cheerleader, my everything. At one point in the aftermath of my father's sickness and death, I was so upset with God that I stopped praying. Full of anger, I broke my silence only to yell at God. And do you know what? God listened patiently to me. And so I talked to God some more the next day and then the next day.

Trusting God amid sorrow and suffering is difficult. Even now, I still have days when it is hard to get out of bed or when I feel like a hamster on a wheel – going through the motions, oblivious to my surroundings. Starting my mornings with prayer, a devotional and some scripture helps to keep me centred. My heartache remains, but with time and God's help, the pain of losing my dad has numbed and my relationship with God has grown.

Loss brings anger, confusion and frustration. But my experience has taught me that God is with us – through big and small things. Our creator is strong enough for our anger and patient enough for our questions.

Prayer: *Dear God, we trust you with today and our tomorrows. Guide our paths, our decisions and our hearts. Amen*

Thought for the day: God is strong enough to handle my anger.

Patty Sears (Indiana, USA)

Showing appreciation

Read 1 John 3:16–18

Dear children, let us not love with words or speech but with actions and in truth.
1 John 3:18 (NIV)

My entire adult life has been dedicated to my wife, our four children and now our grandchildren. I took my family camping, coached Little League and drove a station wagon. I showed my love for my children in the best way I knew how – by spending time with them. My kids now live all over the country and have careers and their own families, and I miss them greatly.

One day I ended up in A&E, and two days later I needed triple bypass open-heart surgery. I went under anaesthesia knowing that my wife and friends were praying in the waiting room. Neither my wife nor I knew that all four of our children had dropped everything to travel hundreds of miles to be there. When I woke up in the recovery room, I was surrounded by more love than I ever hoped to receive. My children demonstrated their love for me just by being present. I felt overwhelmingly appreciated, and that bleak October day turned into the best day of my life!

When I consider how loved I felt that day, I think of how God must feel when we set aside time for prayer and praise. Showing sincere gratitude is one way we can show our love for God.

Prayer: *Ever-present Father, thank you for always being here with us. Call us daily to spend time with you. Amen*

Thought for the day: I show my appreciation to God when I take time to be present.

Chris Grove (Oklahoma, USA)

Stronger than before

Read 2 Corinthians 4:7–16

So we do not lose heart. Even though our outer nature is wasting away, our inner nature is being renewed day by day.
2 Corinthians 4:16 (NRSV)

I was driving my daughter home from school when we got stuck in traffic due to road maintenance work. I was in a hurry, so I complained: 'What have they done to the road? They've dug such big holes that we can't even get through.' In response to my complaints, my daughter asked, 'Mama, if they don't dig and break the road, then how will they make it new?'

This statement made me think about how similar our Christian life is. When we go through difficult situations and unwelcome seasons, we feel broken and shattered. In those moments we often question God. We forget that in our brokenness, God can mould and shape us and ultimately bring us back to the path we need to be on. God will rebuild us even stronger than before. Our experiences can then become a testimony so that others may also have hope. Even when it feels like we are being broken, God is always building us up.

Prayer: *O God, make us into the people you want us to be. When we feel broken, give us hope as we pray, 'Father, hallowed be your name, your kingdom come. Give us each day our daily bread. Forgive us our sins, for we also forgive everyone who sins against us. And lead us not into temptation.'* Amen*

Thought for the day: My experiences strengthen my faith and give hope to others.

Manasi Mohanty (Odisha, India)

PRAYER FOCUS: CONSTRUCTION WORKERS
*Luke 11:2–4 (NIV)

When words fail

Read Romans 8:22–27
The Spirit himself intercedes for us through wordless groans.
Romans 8:26 (NIV)

Just as the world was shutting down due to Covid-19, I learned that I had aggressive prostate cancer that required immediate surgery. Fear overwhelmed me. I wondered if I could even receive treatment in the midst of a pandemic. The prayers of friends lifted me, yet my own praying was, in the words of Franciscan Richard Rohr, both 'constant and impossible'.

In late afternoons during my days of waiting, I walked by the river and along tree-lined streets near my home. I babbled my prayers but soon ran out of words. Finally, I prayed, 'Father, I have no more words. Please let my steps be prayers and my breath be praise.' I remembered how Paul wrote that the Spirit prays with us and for us when we can manage only groans and sighs. My anxiety did not disappear; but I began to see beyond it as I walked and breathed. My mind became calm as it no longer grasped for words. I began to see and hear the birds along the river. I noticed the sunlight through the trees. I saw other people walking – no doubt bearing burdens of their own.

Eventually I had successful surgery, and I give thanks for caring doctors, nurses and other dedicated healthcare workers. Most of all I give thanks for God's Spirit that sustains. And I continue to pray – sometimes with words.

Prayer: *O God, you know our needs before we ask. Hear us when we pray with words and without them. Amen*

Thought for the day: I don't always need words to pray.

Kevin Horne (Louisiana, USA)

Unclaimed blessings

Read 1 Chronicles 4:9–10

*'Do not be afraid, little flock, for it is your Father's good pleasure
to give you the kingdom.'*
Luke 12:32 (NRSV)

When I worked as an airline service agent, I would frequently help people find their missing luggage. However, I noticed that over time, the airport accumulated suitcases and personal belongings that were left behind. Those items would sit in our storage area, sometimes for months, unclaimed by anyone despite our efforts to alert other airports and airlines worldwide. It seemed as if no one had ever filed a missing baggage report. And the owners never got the pleasure of being reunited with those personal effects, some of which appeared to be quite valuable or sentimental.

I thought of those unclaimed items as I read 1 Chronicles and wondered, 'Do we sometimes miss out on God's blessings because we fail to ask?' Perhaps we think we are undeserving or insignificant. But the book of James says that whatever we lack might be because we don't ask or we ask wrongly (James 4:2–3).

In today's reading, Jabez was not hesitant about asking God to bless him in very specific ways, and God granted his requests. I want to be bold like Jabez. I want to confidently ask God to bless me. I want to believe that my creator desires to bless me lavishly. All the while, I hope to remember that all blessings are given in accordance with God's will and divine purpose.

Prayer: *Dear Lord, thank you for all the ways that you bless us. Help us to speak the desires of our hearts to you and trust in your purpose. Amen*

Thought for the day: I can ask God for my heart's desires.

Arlene Henry (St. Maarten)

Choosing our perspective

Read Romans 8:31–39

I am convinced that neither death nor life… neither height nor depth, nor anything else in all creation, will be able to separate us from the love of God that is in Christ Jesus our Lord.
Romans 8:38–39 (NIV)

After seeing several physicians, I finally received my diagnosis. Sitting next to my mum in the tiny office, the doctor told me that the tests and consultations were conclusive. I had non-Hodgkin's lymphoma.

I remember feeling a great sense of hope and determination. Fear could have taken root, but I decided that God was greater than any sickness I could face – even cancer. I trusted that, whatever the outcome, God still loved me.

During that summer of treatment, I stayed in the Philippines with my mum while I finished the last of my required college classes online. Some days were uncomfortable while other days felt mediocre, but I pushed through knowing that each day I visited the hospital was a new day of grace and mercy.

Nine years later, I remain in remission. My journey taught me that we can choose how we approach challenges. It also showed me that the love of God is far more powerful than any sickness, doubt, worry or fear.

When we face challenges, we can choose to see them as opportunities to remember God's faithfulness. And if we can't remember specific moments from our lives, we can always recall God's ultimate act of love in sending Jesus.

Prayer: *Dear God, thank you for your unconditional love. Help us to remember your faithfulness when we face challenges. Amen*

Thought for the day: What is one way God has been faithful in my life?

Jamae (Oregon, USA)

Rejection and acceptance

Read Psalm 66:16–20

The Lord said to Samuel, 'Do not consider his appearance or his height, for I have rejected him. The Lord does not look at the things people look at. People look at the outward appearance, but the Lord looks at the heart.'

1 Samuel 16:7 (NIV)

I enjoy tinkering with words. There is no better feeling than when a piece I have written is accepted by an editor, and it hurts to receive a rejection notice. But that hurt is nothing compared to the hurt we feel when rejected by someone we know.

We all are different. Yet, deep inside each of us is the desire to be accepted. We want to fit in, we want to be heard and we want to be understood. I am an imperfect Christian. I remember times when I have not accepted or understood people in my encounters. I'm sure my rejection hurt them.

Jesus loved people who were rejected by society. He demonstrated for us how we should live – especially when we encounter a person who is struggling to find acceptance. The last sentence in 1 Samuel 16:7 offers time-tested wisdom: 'People look at the outward appearance, but the Lord looks at the heart.'

As we look to improve our hearts and our interactions with people who are searching for acceptance, we can be encouraged by Psalm 66:20: 'Praise be to God, who has not rejected my prayer or withheld his love from me!'

Prayer: *Father of us all, help us to see people's hearts and not just their outward appearance. Help us to love like Jesus. Amen*

Thought for the day: I can offer God's gift of acceptance to each person I meet.

Bill Pike (Virginia, USA)

Patiently trusting

Read Colossians 3:12–17

The end of a matter is better than its beginning, and patience is better than pride.
Ecclesiastes 7:8 (NIV)

Renovating a house can be fun, but it can also be a test of patience. My husband is an experienced carpenter, so he is able to do most of the renovations. I am not a professional decorator, but I know what I want. Sometimes it creates friction between us when he has a vision in his head and I have a picture scribbled on paper. He tries his best to create what I want. Sometimes as I observe the process, I wonder if he really understands my vision. But if I wait long enough, my husband does get it right. Although it can be a challenge, I am learning to trust more and control less.

'Trust more and be patient' is probably a good approach for other areas of my life as well. I still make foolish choices, and sometimes my decisions are not exactly what God would want me to do. But God is patient and kind. And God loves and forgives me. I've discovered that if I trust that God is in control, it's easier to be more patient. When I do that, God has this remarkable way of bringing all things to fruition.

Prayer: *Dear God, you know our weaknesses and our eagerness to get things done. Teach us to have patience and to trust you in all areas of our lives. Amen*

Thought for the day: Today I will try to control less and trust God more.

Glynis M. Belec (Ontario, Canada)

Still creating

Read Psalm 8:1–9

God saw every thing that he had made, and, behold, it was very good.
Genesis 1:31 (KJV)

While I don't consider myself to be an expert on gardening, I do enjoy my small planter and border flower gardens. I read about how to maintain my plants, and I try to keep them free of weeds and watered according to their needs. It occurred to me one day as I saw the beginnings of some blooms on my angelonia that through that plant, I was given the gift of watching God in the creation process.

For most of my life, I have thanked God for the things God has created – the earth, its plants and animals, the universe – with the mentality that it is all past. But as I watched my plants blooming, I realised that God is still creating.

I find new blessings when I see a colourful sunset, a falling star, a lunar eclipse, healing within a troubled family or a new start after forgiveness. A multitude of blessings surround me as God's creation continues. And, as God said in Genesis, 'It is very good.'

Prayer: *Dear God, we pray that your Holy Spirit will keep us aware of the creation that continues to flourish around us. Help us remember that 'it is very good'. Amen*

Thought for the day: When I care for creation, I join in God's creative work.

Jerry Browning (Arizona, USA)

It's a journey

Read Matthew 18:15–22

As iron sharpens iron, so one person sharpens a friend.
Proverbs 27:17 (CEB)

Becoming a member of the physical wellness group at my church has been an eye-opening experience. Sometimes I have felt isolated in my lifelong battle to eat more healthily and moderately. Yet as I listened to others share their stories, it became evident that I was not alone.

One woman shared her daily effort to avoid foods that triggered her acid reflux. Another spoke of her addiction to sugary snacks. Yet another told us about her ongoing battle with bulimia. Each of us wrestled with feelings of shame, guilt and failure. But as we shared our struggles and searched God's word together, we learned that we can bring our broken-ness to Jesus and trust him for change. And we vowed to support one another in the process.

Among other things, we learned there is no quick fix in the struggle to change. It is a journey, one we walk daily with Jesus. Our individual temptations may vary, but all sin separates us from God and makes us feel alone and ashamed. The gift of the church is that we can gather as a community of sinners and find encouragement, accountability and a place to feel connected.

Prayer: *Heavenly Father, give us the courage to share our burdens with others. Give us the wisdom and love to help those who are in need. Amen*

Thought for the day: God does not want me to struggle alone.

Teresa Todt (Illinois, USA)

Rejoice!

Read Philippians 4:4–9

Rejoice in the Lord always. I will say it again: rejoice! Let your gentleness be evident to all. The Lord is near.
Philippians 4:4–5 (NIV)

The year 2020 was a hard year for everyone. In my country we experienced turmoil not only because of the Covid-19 pandemic, but also because of political unrest, which we are still experiencing. Every day seems a nightmare, and I feel little peace in my heart.

I can relate to the apostle Paul in his letter to the Philippians. He was in prison, and the church in Philippi was worried about him. He used a form of the word 'rejoice' 13 times. Why would he speak of joy when he may have been about to die? For Paul, joy and comfort came from the Lord: 'Rejoice in the Lord always.' Even in the toughest situations God is near us, and that nearness gives us comfort and joy.

I have experienced a number of challenging situations: I failed the CPA exam twice; the university I was working with closed; my parents both work at a bank and thus are at higher risk of Covid-19 exposure. However, Paul's words remind me to rejoice – even in these stressful times – because no matter what, Jesus is still our Saviour.

Even though we experience pain and suffering, God remains faithful. We can find joy in that truth. And in our rejoicing, God gives us *shalom* – peace.

Prayer: *O Lord, your peace transcends all understanding. May our eyes be fixed on your Son, Jesus, the Prince of Peace. Amen*

Thought for the day: Even in difficult times, God is faithful to bring me joy.

Sergio Luis Alfonso (Bulacan, Philippines)

Hollow trees

Read Galatians 6:1–5

Bear one another's burdens, and in this way you will fulfil the law of Christ.

Galatians 6:2 (NRSV)

One sunny autumn afternoon, my adult son and I hiked through a local forest. We stopped at a tree that had a large hollow near the ground. When I stuck my head inside the hollow, my son cautioned that animals might be living in there; but it was completely empty. We were amazed that even with its core missing, the outer part of the tree remained strong.

Similarly, even when people appear stable and strong, they may have a broken heart or troubled soul. One Sunday our pastor invited us to pray with someone near us. I was sitting next to a woman with whom I frequently have casual conversations, and I asked if she needed prayer. Her face crumpled in pain as she said, 'Pray for my daughter – for our relationship.' It was a rare moment of vulnerability when a private heartbreak was revealed.

People I cross paths with each day may be like hollow trees. I am rarely given a chance to peer into the hollow and offer grace or support. Further, I am rarely vulnerable enough to reveal my own hurts and heartbreaks to others. But as part of God's love for us all, God encourages us to look into the hollows in ourselves and others and to respond with love.

Prayer: *Dear God, help us to bear one another's burdens – to give others a space to reveal their hurts and concerns, and to trust enough to reveal our burdens to others. Amen*

Thought for the day: God encourages me to share my burdens with others.

Susan Wakefield Dal Porto (Illinois, USA)

Worth sharing

Read Isaiah 41:6–10

Cast all your anxiety on him, because he cares for you.
1 Peter 5:7 (NRSV)

As a high school student, I am used to coming home and hearing the same question from my parents: 'How was your day?' I usually respond with something superficial, like 'Good' or 'Fine'. I tend to keep the details to myself because I feel like they're not worth sharing. I often forget that my parents don't ask because they want to hear an exciting story. Rather, they ask because they care about me.

I notice this tendency in my prayer life too. I often neglect to tell God how I'm doing because I feel that my struggles are insignificant compared to the hardships others are experiencing around the world. But when I do this, I ignore the fact that God wants a relationship with me. God wants to know what's causing me pain or what's weighing on my heart. God even wants to hear about my day.

First Peter 5 encourages us to cast our anxieties on God, because God loves us and wants to hear our personal thoughts and struggles. This isn't to say that we shouldn't pray for the world or other people. We are also called to love others and pray for them.

Prayer: *Dear God, thank you for your never-ending love. Help us to trust that you want to hear our thoughts and concerns. Amen*

Thought for the day: I will tell God about my day today.

Olivia Orr (Arkansas, USA)

Resurrection hope

Several years ago I attended the memorial service of a colleague who had died. We went around the room for a time of sharing. One of my colleagues, when it came his turn, said, 'I will miss her, but I will see her again.' I'd heard that sentiment on similar occasions and often dismissed it as a platitude. But something about it struck me differently this time. Perhaps it was his manner, his confidence or the statement's hopefulness even though nothing about the situation seemed particularly hopeful.

As I sat through the rest of the service, I started thinking about the resurrection – an event I tend to take for granted and only focus on once a year. My Christian upbringing and my education had equipped me to think about it abstractly, and I was still very much in my head about it. However, after hearing, 'I will miss her, but I will see her again,' I started to pay attention to the ways the hope of resurrection changed the people around me and the ways it changed me. I started to see how it changed that moment of grieving and how we experienced the tragedy of our colleague's death. We were gathered to grieve but also to remind each other of our hope. I could also perceive the change beyond the sanctuary's walls, out in the world. Resurrection was no longer only an event that happened 2,000 years ago but a very tangible reality that continues to transform me and the world around me. Everywhere I looked there was sadness and pain. And everywhere I looked there were also signs of hope.

I will miss her, but I will see her again. Though the statement didn't take away my grief, it changed my response. It reminded me that sometimes things are bad – really bad – and that's not the end. Grief is ongoing but so is hope, and the two can – and often do – exist in us at the same time. Even when I don't feel hopeful, hope persists.

More than the moment in history that changed everything, resurrection is our reality. It's the moment that changes us. It is the hope that dwells in us. I love that some aspects of hope remain mysterious and leave me awestruck in much the same way that I imagine it did those who encountered Jesus after his death. For me resurrection hope is a different kind of hope than what I experience in my day-to-day life. Resurrection hope transcends my emotions and anything I might be feeling at any point in time. Sometimes I feel very hopeful. Sometimes I don't feel any hope at all. But the hope is still there in the deepest grief and sharpest pain, and I have it whether or not I actually feel it right now. And nothing can take it away.

After Jesus is crucified, we find Mary Magdalene and the other Mary sitting in front of the tomb (see Matthew 27:61). It's a wonderful image and one that I can relate to, having myself sat in front of several tombs – literal and figurative. The sense of finality is overwhelming, the moment almost too much to bear. Then, a few verses later, the earthquake. And the angel says to them, 'Tell his disciples, "He has been raised from the dead, and... he is going ahead of you to Galilee; there you will see him"' (Matthew 28:7, NRSV). The story continues: 'They left the tomb quickly with fear and great joy, and ran to tell his disciples' (v. 8). As we begin to turn our attention towards the season of Pentecost, I think this is a good scene to end on: the two Marys running to share the news of Jesus' resurrection. They were joyful though they hadn't yet seen Jesus. They only had the assurance that they would. I understand their fear. With regard to my own losses, wounds that won't seem to heal or impossible situations, there is always fear. But resurrection hope means there can also be joy. And many days, that is enough for me.

QUESTIONS FOR REFLECTION

1 When has it been most difficult for you to be hopeful? What signs of hope do you see around you today?

2 What does it mean to you to live in joy and hope? Name three small ways that you can live in joy and hope in the days ahead.

3 Read Matthew 28. What do you notice in the narrative that you have not noticed before? Had you been among those to see Jesus after his resurrection, what do you think that experience would have been like?

Andrew Garland Breeden, acquisitions editor

The vine that bears fruit

Read John 15:1–9

'I am the vine, you are the branches. Those who abide in me and I in them bear much fruit, because apart from me you can do nothing.'
John 15:5 (NRSV)

When my husband and I moved to the countryside, we wanted to plant a vineyard and make small batches of wine. So we consulted a local winemaker who recommended varieties of grapes for our climate; we carefully planted the vineyard; we set out a drip line, constructed support wires and pruned the grapevines. We worked for five years but couldn't get anything to grow. The grapes would form and then wither in the summer heat.

Along with the grapes, we also planted a couple of blackberry bushes. They loved the soil, the water we lavished on the vineyard and the climate. Before long, we had rows of productive blackberry bushes. One summer we harvested 200 cups of fruit! Eventually we let their vines take over the grapes.

I realised how much life is like our vineyard. We make plans and envision a future, but often we encounter God in the unexpected – in the blackberry bushes. If we stubbornly stick to our plans, we may miss the opportunities God places in front of us.

Prayer: *Dear God, thank you for your bountiful gifts. Help us to see your guiding hand at work in our lives so that we can know that you are the true vine and our source of life. Amen*

Thought for the day: I gain perspective when I let go of my plans and look for God.

Kathryn Jones Malone (Texas, USA)

Music in the mundane

Read Psalm 118:19–24

This is the day that the Lord has made; let us rejoice and be glad in it.
Psalm 118:24 (NRSV)

I was washing breakfast dishes when I heard enthusiastic chirping right outside my window. Having lived in the heart of the Philippines' busiest city for over 30 years, I was surprised to hear birds nearby. 'Where did they come from?' I wondered as I strained to catch a glimpse. Then it dawned on me: the usual cacophony of traffic and subsequent pollution had recently lessened due to nationwide restrictions. The result was a cleaner, more peaceful environment. So the birds were back! And their chatter was so delightful that I stayed in that spot longer than necessary just to listen.

Clear skies and peaceful streets invited the birds on our rooftop and with them came a new song that brought joy and delight to this weary city dweller. As I made this connection and listened to the birds, I realised how often fatigue, confusion and doubt can pollute our minds and block out the joy. But scripture can break through and renew our mind and spirit. When we seek God, our creator will refresh us and show us that every ordinary day is something special.

Prayer: *Dear Lord, thank you for reminding us that this is the day you have made. Help us to rejoice and be glad in it. Amen*

Thought for the day: God can use the ordinary to reveal the extraordinary.

Kitty Espiritu-Ricafort (Manila, Philippines)

A complete stop

Read Exodus 20:8–11

There remains, then, a Sabbath-rest for the people of God; for anyone who enters God's rest also rests from their works, just as God did from his.
Hebrews 4:9–10 (NIV)

As we were driving one day, my wife reminded me that a stop sign means *stop*, not *slow down*. God's sabbath also asks us to stop and cease all work. Just like my driving skills, I am good at slowing down for the sabbath. But I am not great at completely stopping when it comes to daily and weekly tasks. Sometimes I consider slowing down for sabbath as good enough or meeting the basic requirements. Yet that is not what God instructs us to do.

God designed the sabbath and invites us to rest because God loves us. It is a gift to restore our mind, body and entire being. It also reminds us that life is about more than completing tasks. Sometimes the sabbath feels counterintuitive because we think that stopping keeps us from being productive. But rest helps us avoid burnout, have sharper minds and complete the tasks God gives us to the best of our ability.

Prayer: *God of rest, thank you for your healing sabbath. Help us to remember to stop in the midst of our busyness in order to renew our perspective and strength in you. Amen*

Thought for the day: Sabbath rest is a gift from God.

Milan P. Winters (Florida, USA)

Wherever we go

Read Joshua 1:1–9

The Lord is my light and my salvation – whom shall I fear? The Lord is the stronghold of my life – of whom shall I be afraid?
Psalm 27:1 (NIV)

Our church decided to embark on a new ministry programme teaching English as a second language. My job was to interview prospective students. After asking them where they had come from, I asked what they missed about their home country. I'll never forget speaking with one young woman from Bolivia. As her eyes filled with tears, she haltingly said that she missed her mother and father and her family. Then she said wistfully, 'I miss the mountains.' At that moment I realised what this woman had given up in leaving her native land.

In our scripture today, we read that Moses had passed away and that God told Joshua that it was now his job to lead the Israelites to the promised land. For some of them, they would be leaving the only home they had ever known. God told Joshua, 'Be strong and courageous. Do not be afraid; do not be discouraged, for the Lord your God will be with you wherever you go.'

Whether we are moving to a new place, a new job or a new school or reordering our life to begin on a more spiritual foundation, we too have the assurance that God is with us. And knowing that gives us courage to move forward.

Prayer: *Dear Lord, thank you for being with us always. Help us to cast our cares upon you, especially during times of change and transition. Amen*

Thought for the day: I will let God be my guide, this day and every day.

Martha Knobel Maxham (Maryland, USA)

God celebrates us

Read Psalm 103:1–12

Like a parent feels compassion for their children – that's how the Lord feels compassion for those who honour him.
Psalm 103:13 (CEB)

I once had the opportunity to watch my teenage son playing bass in a band. During the performance, my attention never left the bass player! I was completely in awe of him. After they finished one song, my wife and I applauded enthusiastically with a handful of other people. Of the many people in attendance, only a handful applauded. Perhaps those applauding were the parents of the six teenagers on stage. The boys' playing was not that good, but that didn't diminish my interest in my son's playing. Whether he plays the instrument properly or not, I am still eager to hear and watch him play because I love him.

That's how God feels about us. Whether or not we become famous, successful or smart or achieve great things, God is still interested in our lives because God loves us. God loves us not because we are good at things or even because we are good. God loves us simply because we are children of God.

Prayer: *Thank you, Father, for celebrating us as your children, not because we are worthy but because you love us. In the name of Jesus Christ we pray, 'Father, hallowed be your name, your kingdom come. Give us each day our daily bread. Forgive us our sins, for we also forgive everyone who sins against us. And lead us not into temptation.'* Amen*

Thought for the day: God loves me no matter what I do.

Jonson Siahaan (Indonesia)

Mission opportunities

Read James 5:13–16

Be alert and always keep on praying for all the Lord's people.
Ephesians 6:18 (NIV)

As a nurse I ride the hospital elevator often, and each day before going to my floor I pray for visitors who will use the same elevator. Most visitors are not happy about being at the hospital. Some have travelled long distances, worried and concerned for a loved one.

When I enter the elevator, I always smile and ask, 'How is your day going?' With these five words I can enter people's lives, and God's work can begin. Some will simply smile and politely say, 'Fine. How is your day?' But sometimes the conversation goes deeper. Responses I have heard include: 'My day is not good; my husband had a stroke, and he is not doing well' or 'I am so tired; I haven't slept in days since my son was brought here after the accident.' The elevator ride is quick, so I can only offer brief responses: 'I am so sad to hear that this is happening to your loved one. I will pray for both of you today.'

We don't need a passport or a plane ticket to go on a mission trip. Mission opportunities are all around us. With God's help we can find ways to share love and compassion with the people we encounter each day. It will be a rewarding experience.

Prayer: *Holy God, help us to look for opportunities each day to serve those who need to feel your love. Amen*

Thought for the day: Opportunities to offer love and compassion are all around us.

Cheryl A. Mart (Texas, USA)

Putting God first

Read 1 Peter 5:6–11

'Other seed fell among thorns, which grew up and choked the plants.'
Matthew 13:7 (NIV)

It had been a stressful workday, and I was very distracted on my way home. While I was waiting at a traffic light, a truck pulled up behind me and honked. I glanced in the rearview mirror but did not immediately recognise the vehicle. As I waited for the light to turn green, the truck honked several more times.

Once the light turned green and we began moving, the truck switched lanes and started to pass me. I looked over and saw the driver smiling and waving at me! He was someone I knew, and he was just honking to be friendly. I simply had not been paying attention.

During the rest of my drive home, I wondered how many times in my life I have not listened when God tried to get my attention. All too often I have allowed stress to distract me and block out God. My concerns are significant, but it is a problem when I allow my cares to be a higher priority than God. Peter tells us to 'cast all your anxiety on [God] because he cares for you' (1 Peter 5:7). Rather than worrying, I can give my cares to God.

Prayer: *Merciful and loving God, help us to put the events of life in the proper perspective. You are first; everything else is second. In Jesus' name. Amen*

Thought for the day: 'Cast your cares on the Lord and he will sustain you' (Psalm 55:22).

Chuck Hudspath (Illinois, USA)

Finding direction

Read Psalm 25:4–11
Your word is a lamp to my feet and a light to my path.
Psalm 119:105 (NRSV)

When I began using a smart-watch fitness tracker I'd received from a friend, I faced two obstacles: figuring out how to charge it and synchronising the watch with my smart phone so they could share data. Because my friend had misplaced both the original packaging and the instruction manual, I went online hoping to find the answers I needed. To my dismay, nothing on the watch indicated what brand or model it was. It wasn't until the original owner sent a product description that I realised it was a completely different brand than I had thought. However, once I entered the correct information, the synchronisation process was easy.

How often we try to figure things out ourselves, without seeking God's direction! Somehow we end up going in a roundabout way, much like the Israelites did in the book of Exodus when they left Egypt. Just as God provided the navigational tools they needed – a pillar of cloud by day and a pillar of fire by night – God wants to direct the steps of our lives. As we pray, read the Bible and yield to the promptings of the Holy Spirit, God will help us find our way out of the mistakes of our past and enable us to look towards the future with confidence and hope.

Prayer: *Dear God, thank you for guiding us on this journey called life, and for the assurance that you will never lead us astray. Amen*

Thought for the day: I can stay on course when I keep in step with God.

Arlene Timber-Henry (St. Maarten)

Childlike faith

Read 1 Corinthians 13:8–13

When I was a child, I spoke like a child, I thought like a child,
I reasoned like a child; when I became an adult, I put an end to
childish ways.
1 Corinthians 13:11 (NRSV)

'Who do you want to be when you grow up?' My dad asked me that question throughout my childhood. My six-year-old self responded, 'I want to be a veterinarian.' 'No,' my dad would say. 'That's what you want to *do*. I asked, "Who do you want to *be*?"' As a child, I equated having a particular job with who I would become. Now I understand how those things are different.

Reflecting on this made me think of other 'childish ways'. Have I put them behind me? Is my identity rooted in a title or a position? Do I long for notoriety? Do I still throw tantrums? God wants all of us to come to Jesus with *childlike* faith, but that's different from *childish* faith.

Recently I met a six-year-old boy, Aiden. Following in the footsteps of my dad, I asked Aiden, 'Who do you want to be when you grow up?' He replied, 'I want to be a man.' His response was childlike but not childish. It was said with the innocence of a child who simply wants to grow and mature – to become the person God created him to be. Aiden's answer reminds us all that rather than focusing on what we do or how we can make a name for ourselves, we can focus on becoming who God has created us to be.

Prayer: *Dear Lord, give us a faith that is childlike but not childish.*
Help us to become the persons you created us to be. Amen

Thought for the day: Who is God calling me to be when I grow up?

Dori H. Gorman (Tennessee, USA)

Time with God's word

Read Isaiah 40:27–31

Those who hope in the Lord will renew their strength. They will soar on wings like eagles; they will run and not grow weary, they will walk and not be faint.
Isaiah 40:31 (NIV)

Several years ago, I began to study the Bible by reading and memorising passages. I tried to retain what I had read, but after a while I couldn't remember. I was frustrated because I felt that my efforts were in vain.

One day I was watching a programme about the Northern Fulmar, a marine bird found in the North Atlantic, North Pacific and Arctic oceans. Fulmars enjoy feeding on crustaceans, squid, jellyfish and scraps generated by fishermen. When baby fulmars leave their nest, they are too heavy to fly, so they float on the water, taking time to digest and lose weight. But other marine life and fishermen take advantage of the situation and capture the vulnerable fulmar.

I reflected on this story and thought of studying the Bible. Bible study is not about 'filling up' on God's word until we can't absorb more information. Rather it is about pondering God's word and allowing it to nurture us and shape our actions. When we allow God to renew our strength through scripture, we will soar like eagles. God wants us to experience the fullness of life, and scripture is our guide to finding God's purpose.

Prayer: *Creator God, nurture us with your life-changing word each day, and help us discern your will for us. In the name of Jesus. Amen*

Thought for the day: Today I will take time to be nurtured by God's word.

Carlos Xavier Soto Serrano (Puerto Rico)

A shelter from fear

Read Psalm 56:1–3

When I am afraid, I put my trust in you.
Psalm 56:3 (NRSV)

As the tornado warning appeared on my television screen, my legs began to shake. I didn't have a shelter or even a place inside my home where I could stand against a powerful storm. Panicked, I rushed into the hallway and fell to my knees, crying and praying that the violent winds would pass me by. Minutes later they had, and my unstable world was made right again.

For many years I've carried this debilitating fear of major storms. As a Christian, I wonder why I can't just put my trust in the Lord as I am supposed to. Doesn't my fear show lack of faith? But fear is a human emotion, and even the strongest Christian experiences it at one time or another.

In Psalm 56, David cries out to God because he fears his enemies. He doesn't hide his need for protection. He isn't ashamed to reach out to God for shelter. He admits he's facing a battle he can't handle on his own. Reading Psalm 56 always calms me.

Though we are children of God, there is much in life that can scare us. Though we put our faith in God, we can't deny our human emotions. But we can reach out to God when we are overwhelmed, hurt or afraid — and we can trust that God will always be there to listen.

Prayer: *Dear God, calm our fears and help us to remember that you are with us. Fill us with the peace that only you can give. In Jesus' name. Amen*

Thought for the day: In the midst of my fears, I will trust God.

Dawn Rachel Carrington (South Carolina, USA)

Songs from the heart

Read 2 Corinthians 2:14–17

Let the message of Christ dwell among you richly as you teach and admonish one another with all wisdom through psalms, hymns, and songs from the Spirit, singing to God with gratitude in your hearts.
Colossians 3:16 (NIV)

Not being blessed with natural musical ability, it was very difficult and frustrating to learn new songs with the praise team at my church every week. Five years ago, I never heard any of these songs and did not understand the reason for worship. Nor did I realise that many of the songs were actually based upon Bible verses or older hymns. At first, performing each week made me anxious and uncomfortable.

But then the Holy Spirit taught me that it is the 'heart of worship' that counts and the message of the song rather than its delivery. Once I stopped focusing on performing perfectly, I realised that music offered as a labour of love and worship is beautiful and pleasing to God.

The purpose of playing music and singing is to praise and worship God. The psalmist says, 'I will praise God's name in song and glorify him with thanksgiving' (Psalm 69:30). We worship aloud to acknowledge our love for God, not to perform or seek admiration for ourselves. The voices and sounds that fill every church around the world are pleasing to God – especially when our hearts and minds are open to the truth and power of scripture contained in the songs.

Prayer: *Lord Jesus, make us instruments of your love and peace through song. Focus our minds, soften our hearts, open our eyes and ears to the truth of your word. Amen*

Thought for the day: I will sing boldly with a faithful heart as an offering to God.

Robert Racine (North Carolina, USA)

Joyfully waiting

Read Psalm 130:1–8

I wait for the Lord, my soul waits, and in his word I hope.
Psalm 130:5 (NRSV)

Before my husband left on a recent trip, he promised our five-year-old son that he would return soon. For the next few days, our son would jump every time he heard the sound of our front gate opening. He would run to me and say, 'Papa came!' Each time I would tell him that it was not his dad but our neighbour who opened the gate. But our son wouldn't get disappointed. He knew that maybe the next time it would be his dad. And after five long days of waiting, it was his dad who opened the gate. Our son's joy knew no bounds as he jumped into his papa's arms.

How I wish to have such faith in my heavenly Father – a faith that joyfully waits, that is confident and determined and that finds what it seeks. When we experience a season of waiting, we can hold on to God's promises and remain steadfast in our faith. Holding on to hope, we can trust in God's love for us and know that our faith is not in vain.

Prayer: *Dear Father, please help us to wait on you joyfully, knowing that you are a faithful and loving God. Amen*

Thought for the day: When I have confidence in God, even my waiting can be joyful.

Elizabeth Livingston (Maharashtra, India)

A rediscovered gift

Read 1 Peter 4:8–11

Every generous act of giving, with every perfect gift, is from above, coming down from the Father of lights.
James 1:17 (NRSV)

After being confined to my home for a week recovering from ankle surgery, church friends asked if I would like to go out for lunch. Although my mobility was limited to a scooter, I immediately accepted. When I rolled out the front door, the winter air blew across my face. It was as if I had never experienced fresh air! It was renewing. On that day, thoughtful friends helped me rediscover a gift I had forgotten.

Each day is a gift from God; but how often do we pause to think about each day as the refreshing new gift it is? We tend to take simple, recurring experiences for granted; that is, until we no longer have them.

Sometimes difficulty, like a bad ankle, helps us think about God's simple blessings. My ankle surgery was a brief setback; but through the kindness of friends, it awakened me to gifts I previously failed to notice or fully appreciate. Each day is a breath of fresh air from God – a time to celebrate all of God's perfect gifts.

Prayer: *Thank you, God, for each new day with all that it offers, and forgive us for failing to notice or fully appreciate it. In the name of Jesus, who gave the greatest gift. Amen*

Thought for the day: What simple joy from God will I give thanks for today?

Robert K. Abel (Maryland, USA)

Clean away the dust

Read 1 John 1:5–10

If we confess our sins, he who is faithful and just will forgive us our sins and cleanse us from all unrighteousness.
1 John 1:9 (NRSV)

It is amazing and annoying how dust can creep into places you don't expect. Recently my husband and I have been doing some home renovations. I was determined that I would protect all our furniture and made sure I had enough plastic to cover everything.

I didn't think about the insides of the kitchen cupboards, though. I figured the contents of the cupboards were safe since they were all behind doors. But renovation dust managed to creep into the crevices. It wasn't until cleanup time that I noticed the thin layer of dust that had permeated.

As I cleaned out my cupboards, I thought about how it wouldn't hurt to give myself a dusting off too. Sin can creep in just like dust. Prayer and confession are good ways to clean away the dust in my life. It was good to stop and think about how God blesses me every day with mercy and grace.

Prayer: *Gracious God, remind us always of how you created and love us. Help us tidy up areas of our lives that don't bring you glory so we can show our gratitude to you. Amen*

Thought for the day: Each day God gives me abundant mercy and grace.

Glynis M. Belec (Ontario, Canada)

Good people

Read Philippians 2:1–11

Give thanks to the Lord, for he is good; his love endures forever.
Psalm 107:1 (NIV)

One day I was waiting at a bus stop when a blind man joined me. We immediately struck up a conversation – mainly about the bus service and how long we might have to wait. But we were enjoying each other's company.

Finally the bus arrived, and I guided him on to the bus. We paid our fares and sat down together. We continued our conversation, this time about life in general. But I was amazed when he said, 'You know, Lady, God is a good God.' For a moment I thought to myself, 'How can a man who has lost his sight say that God is good?' Then he continued, 'It was not until I lost my sight that I realised how many good people make up our world. I thank the Lord every day for those people.'

My encounter with this man taught me a lesson – that I should count my blessings, large or small, every day. God has promised never to leave us alone and to guide our path every step of our way. So now, whatever problem I face, I am comforted by the fact that God and the good people of our world will see me through it.

Prayer: *God of all goodness, thank you for your grace and mercy each day of our lives. May we show our gratitude by offering acts of goodness and grace to those who pass our way. In Jesus' name. Amen*

Thought for the day: Each new day is a good gift from God.

Sylvia Walker (New York, USA)

Standing back up

Read Proverbs 24:15–20

A just man falleth seven times, and riseth up again: but the wicked shall fall into mischief.
Proverbs 24:16 (KJV)

I recently read that Abraham Lincoln failed in business in 1831, suffered a nervous breakdown in 1836 and was defeated in his run for presidency in 1856. Instead of despairing and giving up, he refused to stop trying his best. Consequently, he was elected as the 16th president of the United States of America in 1860.

Everyone experiences failure. Even Christians experience failure in studies, work, relationships, business and family life. Setbacks are not a problem, but allowing them to paralyse our will to go on can be.

Proverbs tells us that a faithful person can fall many times, but we still have the strength to rise up again. We know that we can stand back up after failures because, as Paul writes, we 'can do all things through Christ' and '[Christ's] grace is sufficient' (Philippians 4:13; 2 Corinthians 12:9).

When we fail – whether it is socially, morally, maritally or in ministry – we cannot give up. Rather, let us look for the cause of our failures and trust that God forgives us and gives us the strength to stand up again.

Prayer: *Merciful God, when we fail, give us the strength to stand up again. Amen*

Thought for the day: God's love, not my failure, defines me.

Asamoah Joseph Omono (Greater Accra Region, Ghana)

Keep looking up

Read Psalm 121:1–8

Come, my heart says, seek God's face. Lord, I do seek your face!
Psalm 27:8 (CEB)

While walking my dog I could not help but notice all the things he was missing. With his nose to the ground he was missing an entire world happening around him. Birds were flying closely around him, and squirrels chattered nervously as he walked by completely unaware of their presence.

Then it occurred to me that my dog is not the only one with his head down. God began to show me how often I literally have my head down looking at my phone. Often I am trying to be efficient and return messages or reply to emails, but I still have my head down and am not paying attention to what is around me. During our walk home, I challenged myself to look up and around me more. It was amazing what I noticed. I noticed children playing in the pond nearby, geese flying in the pristine blue sky and new buds forming on the trees. Through this practice God reminded me of one of my favourite scripture passages: 'I lift up my eyes to the hills – from where will my help come? My help comes from the Lord, who made heaven and earth' (Psalm 121:1–2, NRSV).

I cannot possibly notice all of God's creations if I have my head down all the time. Each and every day I need to keep looking up so that I can see all the wonderful things that God is doing in the world.

Prayer: *Dear God, thank you so much for your reminder to keep looking up so that we can notice all that you have created and all that you are doing. Amen*

Thought for the day: Today I will keep looking up for signs of God's presence.

Michelle T. Johnson (North Carolina, USA)

Before they call to me

Read Isaiah 65:20–25

Before they call, I will answer; while they are still speaking, I will hear.
Isaiah 65:24 (CEB)

My sister and I enjoyed a day visit to the Harrogate Flower Show with a coach party. There was no opportunity earlier to buy postcards to send to housebound friends, and we knew we'd be taken straight back to the hotel afterwards, with no shops near.

While walking round the show and admiring the beautiful blooms and inspiring arrangements, we noticed one nursery had a stand with bundles of postcards showing gorgeous flowers, and a notice saying, 'All free – please help yourself!' As expected, there was an advertisement for the nursery on each one, but it was very discreet and the photos of the flowers were so uplifting.

We gladly availed ourselves of their kind gift, and spent a pleasant time on the lawn in the grounds of the show in the afternoon sunshine, sharing our joy in God's creation by writing to those who could not be there personally and assuring them of our prayers for them.

Truly God answered our need before we called!

Prayer: *Father, thank you for the abundance of your creation, including the different colours and shapes of flowers. Help us to share your bounty with others and to preserve creation for those who will follow us. Amen*

Thought for the day: Those who are housebound can share the beauty of God's creation through pictures.

Christine Hay (Scotland, United Kingdom)

A good day to forgive

Read 1 John 2:7–14

The one who claims to be in the light while hating a brother or sister is in the darkness even now. The person loving a brother and sister stays in the light, and there is nothing in the light that causes a person to stumble.
1 John 2:9–10 (CEB)

I was young when I met the person who would become my husband. Unfortunately, my husband's mother and I did not get along, and the tension was evident through her words and actions. This situation affected our marriage, and my husband and I separated. The rift left a deep wound. But after some time, my husband and I reconciled.

Over time, prayer has deepened my faith, bringing me a greater understanding of God's purpose in my life. Prayer has also been central to changes in my relationship with my mother-in-law. She is now in poor health and suffers from dementia. So during my devotional time, I offer prayers of mercy and forgiveness for her. When I do, I can sense the presence of the Holy Spirit.

Praying for my mother-in-law in this way has been liberating for me, and God has blessed me with a profound sense of peace in my heart because 'darkness is passing away and the true light already shines' (1 John 2:8). Every day is a good day to forgive. And every day is an opportunity to live in the light of God's immense love and mercy.

Prayer: *God of grace, open our hearts and minds when we pray, 'Forgive us for the ways we have wronged you, just as we also forgive those who have wronged us.'* Grant us faith and courage to abide by these words. Amen*

Thought for the day: I will forgive others because God forgives me.

Luz Ángela Galeano M. (Valle del Cauca, Colombia)

Change of plans

Read Romans 8:18–30

Many are the plans in a person's heart, but it is the Lord's purpose that prevails.
Proverbs 19:21 (NIV)

I was in my senior year of high school when the Covid-19 pandemic began. In the years prior, I had set high expectations for the conclusion of my high school career. I dreamed of going to prom, of the emotional last day of school and of getting to graduate under normal circumstances. But in 2020, things that so many of us had worked hard for and waited so long for couldn't happen.

I started to fall into a depression, and my anxiety was the worst it had ever been. Every day seemed to get worse and worse, and I felt as though I was moving further away from God. But little did I know that what God had in store for me was going to be so much more than I could have ever imagined.

In the fall, I was actually able to attend college in person. I was scared and anxious as I didn't know what to expect or how I would do under the circumstances. But God led me to an amazing university where I am able to grow and be reminded daily of God's goodness. God has taught me that although our plans may not work out the way we expected, God still has good plans in store for us.

Prayer: *Dear God, thank you for watching over us even in our darkest hours. Help us to be faithful, hopeful and open to your plans for us. In Jesus' name we pray. Amen*

Thought for the day: When my plans change, I trust that God is still with me.

Cree (Texas, USA)

Built to last

Read Ephesians 2:4–10

I praise you because I am fearfully and wonderfully made; your works are wonderful, I know that full well.
Psalm 139:14 (NIV)

I inherited some pieces of wooden furniture from my parents and a great-aunt. I am not sure when they were originally made, but they are solid pieces that are both beautiful and made to last. They contrast drastically with some of the other pieces of furniture in our home that are not made from solid wood but from plywood. Many of these newer items are nice to look at and functional, but I doubt I will leave any of them in my will to give to someone else.

Psalm 139 tells us that we are fearfully and wonderfully made, knit together by God in our mother's womb. There may be times when we feel fragile. However, like my heirloom wooden furniture, we have an inherent strength, durability and beauty. Circumstances may try to declare otherwise. We may hear whispers that we are not going to make it. But we can be encouraged, knowing that we are God's enduring handiwork.

Prayer: *Dear Father, give us confidence when we feel fragile. Remind us that we are made by you, and we are yours. We pray as Jesus taught us, 'Our Father which art in heaven, Hallowed be thy name. Thy kingdom come. Thy will be done, as in heaven, so in earth. Give us day by day our daily bread. And forgive us our sins; for we also forgive every one that is indebted to us. And lead us not into temptation; but deliver us from evil.'* Amen*

Thought for the day: With God, I can stand the test of time.

Kate Carroll (Kildare, Ireland)

PRAYER FOCUS: CARPENTERS
*Luke 11:2–4 (KJV)

Work in progress

Read Revelation 3:15–16

What good is it if people say they have faith but do nothing to show it?
Claiming to have faith can't save anyone, can it?
James 2:14 (CEB)

As I was putting away the dishes this morning, I looked at our spoonula –
a silicone kitchen tool that is a cross between a spatula and a spoon. It's
a mediocre utensil – neither a good spatula nor a useful spoon. This got
me thinking about those times in my faith when I am mediocre.

I am a work in progress and have been ever since I accepted Jesus
into my heart. Sometimes I am on fire and put my faith into action. Other
times, I am lukewarm with one foot in and one foot out. Without being
committed to any particular path, I lose my way. My work, problems and
worries distract me from loving God and loving others.

I once heard that love is a choice we must make every day in order to
keep it alive. Faith is the same way. We have to choose it daily. And when
we choose it, faith changes our beliefs and conduct. We are transformed.
So if our lives do not change in a meaningful way because of what we
choose to believe, our faith falters. As James wrote, 'A person is shown
to be righteous through faithful actions and not through faith alone'
(James 2:24). We must remember every day to choose God and show
the Lord our love.

Prayer: *Lord of love, help us when we become lukewarm. Show*
us the right tools and actions so that we can act out our faith and
demonstrate our love for you. Amen

Thought for the day: How can I choose God today?

Kim Koratsky (Tennessee, USA)

Comfort in loss

Read John 11:28–37
Jesus wept.
John 11:35 (KJV)

'There is nothing more they can do.' When my daughter told me her husband was coming home on hospice, I couldn't find the words to pray. How could I put into words the loss of a young life cut short by cancer? How could I explain the sadness of those who loved him? I felt Jesus couldn't understand my pain.

Then I read the passage where Jesus arrived in Bethany after his friend Lazarus died. Even though Jesus would ultimately raise Lazarus and triumph over death, he sat and wept. Jesus knew the pain that came from the death of a loved one. He knew the sadness from being with others who mourn. Jesus knew the pain I felt and, like me, he cried. Then he dried his eyes and set about comforting others and doing the will of the Father.

Through this loss, I've learned that when I hurt, Jesus hurts. He understands my pain. He doesn't always fix it; sometimes he just sits with me. This knowledge that Jesus understands my grief allows me to lean on him through prayer. I know that Jesus mourned like me and that I will ultimately be reunited with my loved ones in heaven.

Prayer: *Dear Jesus, walk with us through our pain. Help us to take comfort in both your presence and your ultimate victory over death. Amen*

Thought for the day: Jesus sits with us in our grief.

Wendy Couvillon (Louisiana, USA)

The best that we have

Read 2 Corinthians 10:12–18

Then the cloud covered the tent of meeting, and the glory of the Lord filled the tabernacle.
Exodus 40:34 (NIV)

I tend to fall into the trap of comparing myself with others quite easily. Usually I'm comparing my spirituality or level of ministry involvement to that of others. The other day on social media, I came across a photograph that corrected my perspective. The picture was of a breakfast-in-bed tray that a three-year-old daughter had prepared for her mother. It contained two slices of unbuttered raisin bread and a beautiful mug filled with cold water. Not very appetising, to say the least! But the little fingers gripping the sides of the tray were enough to melt any heart.

Exodus 40 describes the building of the tabernacle by the Israelites in the wilderness and the glory of the Lord descending on it. The contrast between this structure and the temple built later by Solomon is striking (1 Kings 6—8). The first was humble compared to the second, but God did not consider it too lowly to inhabit. He came to it in his full glory. Why? Because it was made from the best the people had at that time.

God doesn't need the finest gifts the world has to offer. God wants us to offer the best that *we* have. If that's what we're giving to God, then God is indeed pleased.

Prayer: *Dear Lord, forgive us when we compare ourselves to others. Help us keep our eyes focused on you and to use the gifts you've given us for your glory. Amen*

Thought for the day: It is enough to offer my best to God.

Esther MacDonald (Quebec, Canada)

Unexpected blessings

Read Luke 11:1–10

'Therefore I tell you, whatever you ask for in prayer, believe that you have received it, and it will be yours.'
Mark 11:24 (NIV)

I was raised in a Christian home and my early Christian education taught me the power of prayer. These lessons have stuck with me, and I have adopted different prayer habits through the years.

Unfortunately, I sometimes pray more *for* things than I pray 'Thank you.' Early in my career I prayed for a promotion that I felt qualified for and expected to receive. I did not get the job. I left that organisation to seek other employment and, for a period of time, my thoughts would often wander back to that job, wondering why my prayer had not been answered.

Years later, I am now retired from a career that brought me enjoyment, economic security, opportunities to contribute to society, professional credentials and friendships with people that I would never have known had my original prayer request been granted. I am in awe to now know that God always gives us blessings, even when it sometimes comes in the form of God saying no.

Prayer: *Loving God, thank you for blessing us much more than we deserve. Help us to recognise all the ways that you answer our prayers, especially when you answer in ways we do not hope for or expect. Amen*

Thought for the day: God answers my prayers – sometimes in unexpected ways.

Milton Looney (Alabama, USA)

Signs of God's presence

Read Exodus 3:1–12
Then John gave this testimony: 'I saw the Spirit come down from heaven as a dove and remain on him.'
John 1:32 (NIV)

During the last days of my grandpa's life, my family and I took a break from the hospice centre where he was staying and went for a walk. We went to a nature centre where I noticed some mourning doves flying around us. I remember thinking, 'Maybe God sent these doves to remind us that God is with us and will continue to provide for us even as we mourn.'

When we arrived back at the hospice centre, I still felt anxious and sad, but I was also reassured that God was present. God appeared to Moses through a burning bush, and in a similar way, God appeared to me through the mourning doves and continues to do so today. Whenever I feel intimidated by what God calls me to do, I look for doves to come across my path, and often they do. Seeing them fills me with peace. I am reminded that God is with me and will provide what I need.

God gives us physical reminders of God's presence. If ever we feel distant from our creator, all we have to do is look around to be reminded of God's love for us.

Prayer: *Ever-present God, thank you for reminding us of your love in physical ways. Give us eyes to see the signs and wonders you place in our paths. Amen*

Thought for the day: I trust that God is always by my side.

Kathryn Agnello (New Jersey, USA)

Slow to anger

Read Ephesians 4:25–32

The Lord is compassionate and gracious, slow to anger, abounding in love.
Psalm 103:8 (NIV)

I was driving home from work one day when another car cut into my lane, almost hitting me. I became furious and wanted to make the driver stop so that I could express my anger. Then I remembered the above scripture verse. I pulled over on the shoulder of the road and prayed, 'Thank you, God, for helping me control my anger before it caused more trouble.' What I intended to do could have caused an accident or unnecessary harm.

Acting on anger often leads to undesirable outcomes and regrets. It is easy to say and do things we don't mean when we're angry, and we can hurt others in the process. Sometimes the hurt we cause may never go away or may take years to heal. It is important to keep God's words with us at all times and learn from God to protect ourselves and the people we encounter.

The Bible reminds us many times that God is slow to anger. By trusting God to be present, praying and learning to follow in the footsteps of Jesus, we will be able to calm our anger and live harmoniously with those around us. Thanks be to God.

Prayer: *Heavenly Father, thank you for your presence and for scripture that helps us manage our anger. We pray in the name of our Lord and Saviour Jesus Christ. Amen*

Thought for the day: Because of God's presence, I can control my anger in any situation.

Kong Peng Sun (Singapore)

All play a part

Read 1 Corinthians 12:12–20

Just as each of us has one body with many members, and these members do not all have the same function, so in Christ we… have different gifts, according to the grace given to each of us.
Romans 12:4–6 (NIV)

As I sat in church, my heart was touched by the sight and sound of the handbell choir. Golden bells, lined up from smallest to largest, sat upon linen-dressed tables. Behind the bells stood white-gloved choir members, poised to lift their bells on cue from their conductor. With precision, each bell pealed with clarity – echoing throughout the church. Together they rang the most beautiful music I had ever experienced. I felt that God must surely be pleased with this joyful noise made 'unto the Lord' (Psalm 98:4, KJV).

It then occurred to me how much the handbell choir is like the church itself – the body of Christ (see Ephesians 1:22–23). The apostle Paul compares the church to the human body and tells us that each member is as important as the others. All play an important role in strengthening and supporting the body of Christ to serve God. And just as the handbell choir needs its conductor to guide them to work in unity, so we need Jesus to guide us.

I now understand that however insignificant we feel our part to be, each role is of great importance to Christ. When we complement the work of others using the gifts given us, we make a joyful and pleasing noise unto our Lord!

Prayer: *Dear Lord, bless us as we serve your kingdom, and strengthen us in our efforts. Give us hearts to encourage one another as we remember that the efforts of all are equally important in your sight. Amen*

Thought for the day: Each person has a part to play in serving God.

Paula May Scott (Florida, USA)

PRAYER FOCUS: SOMEONE NEEDING ENCOURAGEMENT

Birth story

Read Luke 1:57–66

*[Zechariah] asked for a writing-tablet and wrote, 'His name is John.'
And all of them were amazed.*
Luke 1:63 (NRSV)

One day my daughter-in-law asked me to share my son's birth story. In her Native American tradition, birth stories carry particular importance. She knew her own birth story and those of their two daughters, but not her husband's. I realised that I had never told my son this story.

On a fall evening, my wife and I went to the hospital anticipating the arrival of our first child one month early. The next morning, under a clear blue sky, my wife went into labour. She was sedated, but I was present. Soon after delivery, my wife began haemorrhaging. She never regained consciousness, and she passed away six hours later.

The first person to come to the hospital was our pastor, David. Then came my best friend, also called David, and his wife, along with my oldest brother, John. As my wife and I had not chosen baby names, John David seemed appropriate. John means 'God is gracious' or 'gracious gift of God', and David means 'beloved'.

I know God was present at John's birth and grieved at the death of his mother. God surrounded my son with love that day and has continued to love and watch over him. My son now knows that in him God gave the world a beautiful gift.

Prayer: *Dear God, help us to love and trust you even when our situation causes us to question our relationship with you. In the name of Jesus Christ our Saviour and Redeemer. Amen*

Thought for the day: Even when I struggle to comprehend God's love and presence, God is still there.

Ivan W. Nicholson (Minnesota, USA)

Green pastures

Read Matthew 11:25–30

*He makes me lie down in green pastures; he leads me beside still
waters; he restores my soul.*
Psalm 23:2–3 (NRSV)

It was important to me to finish college, but writing my senior thesis
tested my perseverance. When my professor told me that I didn't pass
the class and would have to retake it, I felt like a failure. The thesis class
was expensive. I couldn't pay for it twice and was going to have to ask
my parents for help. I knew that this would be a financial strain – my
mum was already taking in laundry to help my father pay the bills, and
my sister was in college as well.

I felt ashamed that I had to ask for money. And I was anxious and rest-
less about what the future would hold. But one afternoon I opened my
Bible and read from Psalm 23: 'He makes me lie down in green pastures,
he leads me beside still waters; he restores my soul.' I envisioned myself
resting in green pastures with God. Through this scripture and in this
vision, God gave me peace and quieted my soul. The Almighty assured
me that God is in control and knows what I'm going through.

I did end up taking my thesis class again, thanks to the support of my
family. With their help and God's help, I passed the class and graduated
from college.

Prayer: *Dear God, thank you for the divine peace that surpasses
understanding and for the support networks of friends and family that
you bless us with. Amen*

Thought for the day: I can rest with God in green pastures.

Karen Tarine (National Capital Region, Philippines)

God the creator

Read Psalm 8:1–9

'You are worthy, our Lord and God, to receive glory and honour and power, for you created all things, and by your will they were created and have their being.'
Revelation 4:11 (NIV)

The immense scope and minute detail of creation convinces me that there is a God. I read that if the distance between the Earth and the Sun were the thickness of one piece of paper, the distance across our galaxy would be a stack of paper 310 miles high! And then there's the intricacy of the human body: the length of all our blood vessels laid end to end is over 60,000 miles, and the eye is made up of more than two million moving parts!

Science continues to try to explain the *how* of creation, and it's interesting to hear the various theories. But more important to me than the *how* is the *why*. We get a straightforward answer to that when we read the Bible. God created this world to display God's glory. And then, in an embodiment of love, God created us in an image of the divine and gave us life so that we could enjoy creation and worship our creator.

What a gift it is to take pleasure in the breathtaking beauty of God's creation! It's a reminder to take time out of our busy schedules to simply reflect on our remarkable world and worship the Almighty who created it.

Prayer: *Heavenly creator, thank you for the love you express in creation's beauty and for allowing us to be part of it. May we bring honour and glory to you. Amen*

Thought for the day: How do I experience God in creation?

John D. Bown (Minnesota, USA)

One small thing

Read Mark 12:38–44

Calling his disciples to him, Jesus said, 'Truly I tell you, this poor widow has put more into the treasury than all the others.'
Mark 12:43 (NIV)

When I was eleven years old, I was sent to a convalescent home for children because of my severe asthma. The first week, all new patients stayed in the same unit. While there I met a girl named Gladys, who was deaf and had no fingers on one hand.

At that time in the United States, deaf children weren't allowed to use sign language, but she and I would communicate with gestures when the nurses weren't looking. We were only in the same unit for one week; but because of Gladys, as an adult I learned American Sign Language, worked at California School for the Deaf, married a sign language interpreter, raised three deaf foster children and interpreted services in sign language for several churches.

We never know when God can use some small circumstance to make a big difference. I remember how Jesus praised the woman for giving only two coins to the temple treasury because it was all she had to live on. She had no idea people would be inspired by her faithful giving for thousands of years.

God can use our smallest encounters to inspire us to make a big difference for the world and for others, even though we may not know this side of heaven how God does that!

Prayer: *Heavenly Father, help us live faithfully, freely giving what we have for your glory. Amen*

Thought for the day: My small acts of love and faith can show others God is worthy of praise.

Janet Ann Collins (California, USA)

A grateful heart

Read Psalm 92:1–4

I will give thanks to the Lord with my whole heart; I will tell of all your wonderful deeds.
Psalm 9:1 (NRSV)

Returning to work after five weeks of being in isolation due to the Covid-19 pandemic had me grumbling and complaining. The thought of having to wake up early each morning, drive to work and spend eight hours a day at my desk was making me feel disgruntled and irritated.

It was during one of my many moments of grumbling that I remembered that as a Christian I'm called to give thanks to the Lord in every situation, regardless of how I feel. But that's difficult to do. So, here's what I decided: every time I was about to say, 'I don't want to go back to work,' I replaced it with, 'I'm thankful that I have work.' Every time I was about to say, 'I don't want to wake up early,' I replaced it with, 'I'm thankful I have a bed to sleep in.' Wow! What a difference that made! Throughout the week my 'attitude of gratitude' changed my mindset and my perspective towards returning to work. Remarkably, my feelings eventually aligned with what I was saying.

When we find ourselves complaining, we can find something we are thankful for and express our gratitude to God. When we do, our lives can be transformed by living with a grateful heart.

Prayer: *O Lord, change our hearts, and help us to be more thankful to you in all situations. Amen*

Thought for the day: What a difference gratitude to God can make!

Dianne Bradford (Auckland, New Zealand)

Impressions

Read Revelation 14:6–13

'They will rest from their labour, for their deeds will follow them.'
Revelation 14:13 (NIV)

The athletic field was covered with frost as I jogged across it one chilly morning. Glancing back, I saw patterns from my running shoes on the grass. I was reminded of how our lives, the choices we make, also leave marks. For better or worse, our actions make impressions on those around us, and our choices have an immediate effect as well as eternal consequences.

When I first became a Christian, my mentor taught me to always have my spiritual antennae up, even when doing something routine like shopping for groceries. We never know where the Holy Spirit might lead. A kind word spoken in the checkout line might be enough to help raise someone's spirits. Returning a lost phone or wallet to a customer service desk might restore someone's faith in humanity. Helping someone reach an item on an upper shelf might put a smile on their face.

Little things matter to God. As Jesus said, 'Whoever can be trusted with very little can also be trusted with much, and whoever is dishonest with very little will also be dishonest with much' (Luke 16:10). With each faithful choice, we can ensure the impressions we make bring glory to God and benefit others.

Prayer: *Dear God, help us to have our spiritual antennae up at all times. Show us the people in our paths whom we are to love. Amen*

Thought for the day: All my choices are opportunities to be faithful to God.

Rick Stockwell (Connecticut, USA)

The road ahead

Read Proverbs 4:25–27

Let your eyes look straight ahead; fix your gaze directly before you.
Proverbs 4:25 (NIV)

As my five-year-old granddaughter learns to ride her bike without training wheels, she loves to join me on bike rides. I choose safe routes with minimal traffic and watch as she gains confidence in her balance and skill. Yet she still needs verbal reminders to keep her eyes on the road. Every duck, unique rock or pretty flower distracts her. Turning her attention away from the road, she veers off the path, sometimes resulting in near disaster.

I can also become distracted and swerve off course. For example, when I am discouraged, I find myself focusing on the negative things of life. I take my eyes off the road and end up floundering in grief and self-pity, crashing into thorns of despair. Fixing my eyes on God, who is leading the way, helps to keep me on the path.

My granddaughter has my voice to direct her focus back on the road ahead. I've learned that I can also hear the voice of God calling me back to the road when I spend time with God, pray unceasingly, trust God and express gratitude. In God, I always have someone looking out for my best interests.

Prayer: *Dear Lord, thank you for going before us and protecting us even when we don't realise it. Help us to trust in you and hear your voice as you call us back to your path. Amen*

Thought for the day: God is always looking out for my best interests.

Peg Arnold (Colorado, USA)

Loving eyes

Read Luke 15:11–32

Because of his great love for us, God, who is rich in mercy, made us alive with Christ even when we were dead in transgressions – it is by grace you have been saved.
Ephesians 2:4–5 (NIV)

Twice each day I spread rice on the roof of the house to feed the wild birds. The birds gather around to eat and then return later in the evening. One morning while I was sweeping, I noticed a bird with a wounded wing. I brought him into the house to treat his wing, and I gave him a bowl of rice and some water.

I watched as the bird ate, though he was clearly in pain. It made me realise that the Lord also looked at me when I was lost and in pain. God looked at me with loving eyes and helped heal my wounds.

After a week of care, the bird was finally able to flap his wings, although he still couldn't fly. I had to help him join the other birds to eat on the roof. The next day, when I went up to check on him, he was gone. As I looked for him, I heard his singing from the roof. He could fly! Joy and pride filled my heart and gave me a small taste of what the Lord must feel when we return to God's ways.

Prayer: *Loving God, thank you for the way you look at us with love and help us get back on your path. Amen*

Thought for the day: God looks at me with love and cares for me.

Rutman Lumbantoruan (North Sumatra, Indonesia)

Real-life examples

Read Exodus 25:8–30

Make this tabernacle and all its furnishings exactly like the pattern I will show you.
Exodus 25:9 (NIV)

I couldn't imagine how the tabernacle looked by simply reading the instructions God gave Moses in the book of Exodus. But after seeing a life-size reproduction of the tabernacle I understood how the frame, coverings and curtains fit together. Seeing a model helped me understand the instructions God gave Moses.

In the same way, seeing real-life examples of Jesus' parables helps me understand his teachings. I see the tenacity of the persistent widow (see Luke 18:1–8) lived out in a small group as I hear a parent pray for a wayward child year after year. I see the compassion of the good Samaritan (see Luke 10:30–37) lived out in the care local ministries offer to those who need food or shelter.

And when I personally become involved in service activities, I gain even deeper understanding. Then I feel blessed for being a blessing. That's why I contribute to ministries that help people around the world and why I teach, lead and work to reach my community through my local church. By seeing, we understand. And through serving, we experience and show others what scripture means.

Prayer: *Dear God, thank you for the many blessings you have given us. Help us to bless others by sharing our faith with them and caring for them. Amen*

Thought for the day: How might I serve as an example of Jesus' teachings today?

Shirley Brosius (Pennsylvania, USA)

A road map

Read John 14:1–7

Jesus answered, 'I am the way and the truth and the life. No one comes to the Father except through me.'
John 14:6 (NIV)

One of the things that has always intrigued me about my wife is her love for road maps. She learned to read them as a girl, became the navigator for her family and continues to be for ours. Though we often use a GPS now, she still prefers a paper map so she can see the entire course of our journey.

Our lives are like a road trip in many ways. There is a beginning and an end, and how we get between these destinations is important. I don't want to waste my life by getting lost along the way and potentially wasting the precious time I am allotted on earth.

The words of Jesus in John 14:6 remind me how God loves me enough to provide me with a map for life. Jesus invites me into a relationship. But, more than that, Jesus' words and teachings show me the way forward. They help me to live a life that is transformed through a relationship with my creator, who loves me and invites me into eternal life. So I have come to see life as an exciting road trip with Jesus as my guide and strength, helping me day by day!

Prayer: *Our Father, thank you for giving us Jesus as the way, the truth and the life. Walk with us on this journey of life, and transform us to live lives of love modelled after you. Amen*

Thought for the day: When I look to Jesus, I have a road map for life.

Robert Terhune (Oregon, USA)

A step of faith

Read Matthew 14:22–33

Jesus said, 'Come.' Then Peter got out of the boat and was walking on the water towards Jesus.
Matthew 14:29 (CEB)

I have an upcoming medical examination at the hospital that I will be going to alone. Normally, my mother would come with me. So the idea of going by myself fills me with fear and anxiety. 'There might be something terrifying in the test results,' I think. 'When the results do come, will I be able to receive them calmly?'

As I prepare to go by myself, I try to remember Bible stories. I remind myself that I have the support of friends who are praying for me. These thoughts strengthen me. In the midst of this ordeal, I am realising that I need to take a step into the unknown.

When we have something on our minds that we can't stop worrying about, we may brood about it. My experience has taught me about the power of entrusting worry to Jesus. I've heard people say, 'If you take one step forward, Jesus will lead you.' That one step is a step of faith. As we take it, we learn that Jesus walks with us and supports us. With Christ, we are never alone.

Prayer: *Dear Jesus, thank you for walking with us in all situations. Give us the courage to step out in faith and meet you. Amen*

Thought for the day: Sometimes it takes a step of faith to meet Jesus.

Asako Yano (Hiroshima Prefecture, Japan)

Transitions

Read Genesis 37:1–11

We want each one of you to show the same diligence, so as to realise the full assurance of hope to the very end.
Hebrews 6:11 (NRSV)

As I reflect on the days of lifting weights in my youth, I remember how much I hated changing the amount of weight on the bar between lifts. Sometimes the transition between sets took longer than the lifts themselves. But now that I look back, I can see that the transitions had just as much to do with strengthening my body as the lifts did. Each time I pulled the weights off the bar and replaced them with new ones, my hands became tougher and stronger. Every time I twisted and turned with those heavy weights, my abs and obliques were getting toned. Every lift, push, pull and twist during the transition benefited me in the long run.

Throughout the Bible, we also see times of transition. For example, when Joseph had the dream of his brothers bowing down to him, he was not given a royal position the next day. His time of transition lasted many years. But time was needed so he could truly interpret his dreams and learn what it meant to be a good leader. Transitions in life are important – they are God's way of preparing us for what is ahead.

Prayer: *Dear Lord, help us to see that the space between where we are and where we are going is necessary. May the transition make us stronger, wiser and closer to you. Amen*

Thought for the day: God can use my struggles to prepare me for something better.

Henry L. Childress (Arkansas, USA)

In any place

Read Matthew 13:1–9

Preach the word; be prepared in season and out of season; correct, rebuke and encourage – with great patience and careful instruction.
2 Timothy 4:2 (NIV)

One day on the bus ride home the only other passenger was a young man with his pet dog. I sat down beside him. He had a nice smile, and he petted his dog, which he called Milagros, meaning 'miracles'. I found that name interesting, and we started a conversation.

As we talked, I felt inspired to share the good news of Christ's love with the young man, but I was reluctant to follow through. After a while, I decided to speak up. When I did, something changed. The words I spoke were not mine, but God's. It was as if a door had opened that allowed me to share the good news of Jesus with this young man.

I have faith that someday this seed that I planted will bear fruit. The setting – a public transport vehicle – may not have been what I was expecting. But God inspired me to speak in that moment despite my hesitancy and insecurity. God asks us to be willing to do our part, and God will take care of the rest.

Prayer: *Faithful God, help us to move beyond our reluctance and fear and embrace opportunities to share the good news in any place. Amen*

Thought for the day: Every day is an opportunity to plant the seeds of God's love.

Maribel Izquierdo (Valle del Cauca, Colombia)

Unseen divine care

Read Psalm 139:1–6

How precious to me are your thoughts, O God!
Psalm 139:17 (ESV)

While living in Libya, on the edge of the Sahara, I used to take the dog for a walk (or in her case a sniff) around a small, enclosed wooded area near the house.

One day, as I was waiting for the dog, I looked down and saw a large desert ant that was carrying a piece of twig. It was making its way with determination and I was fascinated by this, so I watched silently until it reached its destination. It then laid the twig over the entrance of the nest and tried to push it down. That didn't work, so the ant walked round to the other side and tried again, but once more to no avail. The ant then went down into the nest and pulled on the horizontal twig, again without success.

Very quietly I bent down and slowly reached out and up-ended the twig. Immediately, it was grabbed and disappeared down the hole. I imagined my ant friend saying to the nest that it had just witnessed a miracle!

The episode made me realise how our heavenly Father is always there in the unseen, helping us in ways of which we are unaware. If we could but lift the veil, I am sure we would all be overwhelmed by his love and care over us each day, and by the many heavenly miracles answering our prayer to 'deliver us from evil' (see Matthew 6:13).

Prayer: *Dear God, thank you for your unseen care. Help us to increase our faith.*

Thought for the day: Our God is the all-seeing, all-knowing and all-loving God.

Sheila Holwell (England, United Kingdom)

Building strength

Read Ephesians 6:10–17
Pray without ceasing.
1 Thessalonians 5:17 (KJV)

I had made many visits to various practitioners for my back pain, but nothing was working. This time, the doctor pointed out that while sitting on the exam table, I was slumping over. He told me this was part of the problem, and if I had poor posture all day, I would never get better.

I couldn't instantly fix 30 years of bad posture, but I resolved to try. I monitored my posture throughout the day, while working at my desk, cooking and walking. Week by week, my back pain decreased. It really was that simple! Physical therapy, massages and medication didn't help me, but maintaining good posture made all the difference. After a month, most of my back pain was gone.

Just as I needed to focus on my posture throughout the day to strengthen my back, what if we all focused on God and scripture throughout the day to strengthen our faith? We can memorise a verse and recite it in our minds. We can talk to God about what is going on and what we are struggling with. Scripture is always available, and God is ready to talk whenever we want to.

Prayer: *Dear God, help us to remember that you are our source of life and that we will be rejuvenated if we stay connected to you throughout the day. Amen*

Thought for the day: How will I focus on God and pray more throughout the day?

Christopher L. Scott (Washington, USA)

The bedspread

Read Isaiah 55:8–13

*'My thoughts are not your thoughts, neither are your ways my ways,'
declares the Lord. 'As the heavens are higher than the earth, so are my
ways higher than your ways and my thoughts than your thoughts.'*
Isaiah 55:8–9 (NIV)

When I was young, my mother taught me how to knit and cross-stitch.
These skills have given me many hours of pleasure through the years.
I am now in my 70s, and a friend of mine recently taught me how to
crochet. I started out by making some simple potholders. But after that,
I began crocheting a bedspread of all things!

My friend showed me an intricate pattern that has been used for gen-
erations. When I first started, it just looked like a random group of knots
and twists. Every patch I crocheted seemed mismatched and not very
pretty. But when I stitched the patches together, I saw a beautiful design
that I could not see when I began.

This reminds me of the times in my life when I have experienced challenges. When I am in the middle of challenges, it is impossible for me to
determine a purpose in my situation. I wonder, 'Why is this happening to
me?' But in time, God always shows me a larger picture. As the apostle
Paul wrote in 1 Corinthians 13:12, 'Now we see only a reflection as in a
mirror; then we shall see face to face. Now I know in part; then I shall
know fully, even as I am fully known.'

Prayer: *Dear God, thank you that your thoughts are higher than ours
and for caring for us with your everlasting love. Amen*

Thought for the day: God's ways are always the best ways.

Øystein Brinch (Oslo, Norway)

Remembering God's word

Read Psalm 23

The word of God is alive and active.
Hebrews 4:12 (NIV)

When I was in the fifth grade I attended a one-room country school. Once a year we had Achievement Day with contests for spelling and penmanship, among others. To prepare for the penmanship contest, we were given a poem to practise writing. That year it was Psalm 23. I wrote it over and over, hoping to earn a prize ribbon – but actually gaining something more important.

Years later I was married and expecting my first child. The closer my due date came, the more anxious I felt. I asked God to be with me and for my child to be safe. The night I went into labour I felt a surprising peace. At the hospital Psalm 23 suddenly came to me in its entirety, even though I hadn't read it in years. I had written it so many times back in fifth grade it was in my memory! Now God was using those words to bring me assurance and peace. In that moment I felt God's presence strongly. I knew whether I lived or died that I was in God's care and that everything would be all right.

This experience and Psalm 23 have stayed with me all my life, giving me assurance time and time again. Through the years I have memorised other scriptures, giving God the opportunity to speak through them too.

Prayer: *Dear Heavenly Father, thank you for speaking to us through scripture so that we can feel your presence, guidance and love. Amen*

Thought for the day: Scripture is God's voice speaking to me.

Monna Canida Brauer (Missouri, USA)

Encouraging messages

Read Acts 11:19–30

When [Barnabas] arrived and saw evidence of God's grace, he was overjoyed and encouraged everyone to remain fully committed to the Lord.

Acts 11:23 (CEB)

'Trust in the Lord.' 'You are making a difference.' 'You can count on my prayers for you today.' These notes and many more were written by Craig – one of my co-workers at a Christian ministry – and left on my desk. Other staff members and the men he mentored received similar encouraging messages.

Craig's ardour in edifying others brings to mind Barnabas, the companion of the apostle Paul. Barnabas was renowned for his ability to encourage others. When the church at Jerusalem learned that many Gentiles had become believers in Antioch, they commissioned Barnabas to travel there and instruct them in the faith. Barnabas was excited by the vibrancy of their faith and exhorted them all 'to remain true to the Lord with all their hearts' (NIV). His ministry among them was inspirational. Not only did they remain steadfast in the faith, their testimony resulted in many others coming to Christ.

The body of Christ needs encouragers. Living for Christ can be hard, and trials and difficulties will come our way. Every Christian needs the support of fellow believers to remain steadfast in the faith. How might God work through us to encourage others to grow in their faith?

Prayer: *Dear Lord, thank you for the encouragers in our lives. Please show us how we can encourage someone today. Amen*

Thought for the day: How will I encourage someone today?

Wayne Greenawalt (Illinois, USA)

Enduring care

Read James 2:14–18

Each of you should use whatever gift you have received to serve others, as faithful stewards of God's grace in its various forms.
1 Peter 4:10 (NIV)

I was in shock when, in my late 20s, my life came to an abrupt halt because of a significant injury to my lower back. For months I was confined to bed, unable to manage everyday activities like cooking, cleaning, shopping or going to work. Indeed, I was doing well just to manage my own personal ablutions!

However, during this time God showed me what the body of Christ can do when it puts faith and deeds together in the service of others. Without my requesting it, members of the church I had been attending began arriving with meals, attending to my grocery shopping, gardening, house cleaning and laundry. They drove me to appointments and came by to talk or pray with me. Month after month – indeed for the next few years – faithful people of all ages attended to my physical, social and spiritual needs.

So often we rush to help when people undergo surgery or are recently bereaved, but after a few weeks we get caught up in our busy lives or think there is nothing further we can do or say to help. While some people may only need help for a short time, others need the body of Christ to surround them for months or even years. Perhaps this is something we can all aspire to do for those who need help in our community.

Prayer: *Heavenly Father, thank you for those who faithfully attend to the ongoing needs of others. Help us express our faith through acts of service to one another. Amen*

Thought for the day: What can I do to serve someone's long-term needs?

Bronwyn Ashton Winch (Queensland, Australia)

Sacrifice of thanksgiving

Read 2 Corinthians 9:10–15

I will offer to you a thanksgiving sacrifice and call on the name of the Lord.
Psalm 116:17 (NRSV)

This verse puzzled me the first time I read it. How can thanksgiving be a sacrifice? I thought a sacrifice was supposed to be something difficult. What's so hard about being thankful, and why is it so important?

Years later, I was married and had five children. My days were consumed with motherhood: driving children everywhere, loads of laundry, grocery shopping, cooking. I often felt overlooked and underappreciated. But then one of my children, with no prompting, would say the simple words, 'Thanks, Mum!' That was all I needed and wanted to hear! To be noticed and appreciated by those I love always makes my day.

This is exactly the sacrifice God wants from us. We need to take our eyes off ourselves, take time to acknowledge God and thank God for the innumerable ways he blesses us every day. This is a sacrifice of time and self. It means noticing the many blessings that uplift our lives. It means putting our eyes on God and giving God honour, appreciation and thanks.

Prayer: *Dear God, forgive us when we take you for granted. Create in us a spirit of gratitude and thanksgiving for all you are and all you have done. Amen*

Thought for the day: I will thank God each day for my blessings.

Kelly Mulligan Jamieson (Oregon, USA)

Sunshine after rain

Read Psalm 34:1–8

The Lord is close to the broken-hearted and saves those who are crushed in spirit.
Psalm 34:18 (NIV)

In April 2008, we lost our teenage son, Nick, to suicide. Nick was much loved by our large family and his many friends. His sudden passing left us with raw emotions of shock, loss, anguish and grief. How could this have happened, and why did God allow it? Searching scripture, I discovered Psalm 34. Reading verse 18 brought an immediate conviction in my heart that, as painful as this was, God would take care of us.

The weather forecast for the day of the funeral called for a 100% chance of rain. I offered this short prayer: 'God, I need blue skies and sunshine to bury my son.' On the morning of the funeral, the sky was threatening; but as we emerged from the service midday, the clouds had vanished, the skies were blue and the sun was shining. The weather remained perfect the rest of the day. In the days that followed, we were surrounded by family and friends who cared for all our needs, a further sign of God's continuing compassion.

God did not answer my 'why' question; but God was present, showing compassion, sovereignty and care. We will forever mourn our son, but we will live on with hope and a certainty that God loves us and that we will someday join Nick in eternity.

Prayer: *Dear Father, when we are overcome with grief, thank you for your promise never to leave us. In Jesus' name. Amen*

Thought for the day: God's love will see us through our greatest trial.

Stephen E. Freeman (Virginia, USA)

God's fingerprints

Read 2 Corinthians 1:3–7

Praise be to the God… who comforts us in all our troubles, so that we can comfort those in any trouble with the comfort we ourselves receive from God.
2 Corinthians 1:3–4 (NIV)

My glass-front cabinet holds intriguing items, and each one has a story to go with it. Some of the pieces also catch the attention of toddlers and crawling babies, and I enjoy watching their reactions when they plaster their faces or fingers against the glass. After the parents take their little ones home, I often forget to clean the glass. Later when the sun or a bright indoor light shines on the glass, I see the fingerprints all over it.

This fingerprint evidence left behind for me to find later makes me think of my life. When I am in the middle of difficult times, it is easy to overlook God's fingerprints and involvement in my life. I sometimes question if God hears my prayers, sees my pain or cares about my circumstances. Later, when God's light shines in, I can look back and see that God has been there all along offering guidance, comfort and walking beside me each step of the way.

Prayer: *Dear God, thank you for the guidance and comfort that you give us along each step of life's journey. In Jesus' name we pray. Amen*

Thought for the day: I can see evidence of God's love for me everywhere.

Carol Elaine Harrison (Saskatchewan, Canada)

Praying for others

Read Ephesians 6:18–20

I ask that requests, prayers, petitions, and thanksgiving be made for all people.
1 Timothy 2:1 (CEB)

During a recent stop at a fast-food restaurant, I ordered from a woman wearing a cross necklace made from two nails. When I complimented her on the necklace, she told me that she had been in recovery from addiction for over two years. She said she wore it as a reminder of God's presence in her life.

After thanking her for telling me about the cross, I told the woman that I pray every morning for those in recovery from addiction. Although we were strangers, I had actually prayed for her that morning and would continue to pray for her in the future. She smiled, and I knew God had brought me here for a reason. I could now put a face to my prayers.

In Paul's letter to the Ephesians he urged the church to be alert and always keep praying for God's people. Prayer is one way we show our love for others and support our siblings in Christ. It is time well spent.

Prayer: *Dear Lord, give those who are recovering from substance abuse the strength and support they need for one more day free from drugs and alcohol. Give us compassion for all as we pray, 'Our Father in heaven, hallowed be your name, your kingdom come, your will be done, on earth as it is in heaven. Give us today our daily bread. And forgive us our debts, as we also have forgiven our debtors. And lead us not into temptation, but deliver us from the evil one.'* Amen*

Thought for the day: I will pray for others today.

Michael Gooch (North Carolina, USA)

Follow God's lead

Read Jeremiah 17:7–8

'Blessed is the one who trusts in the Lord, whose confidence is in him.'
Jeremiah 17:7 (NIV)

To celebrate our eleventh wedding anniversary, my husband and I took ballroom dancing lessons – something we had wanted to do for years! Before we learned the basic steps to the foxtrot, waltz and merengue, our instructor taught us proper dancing position. He showed us where to place our hands and told us to imagine we had swallowed broomsticks so we would stand tall and straight. Then he instructed me to let my left shoulder rest firmly in my husband's hand so my husband could easily guide me across the dance floor. Yet, instead of trusting his guiding hand, I often tried to anticipate the next steps or even completely take over, resulting in a misstep and loss of rhythm.

That advice about ballroom dancing has stuck with me because of its broader application. How often do we ignore God's guiding hand and try to guess and plan the best steps forward? How often do we take over, thinking we know best? Yet all the while God is present to guide us if we trust ourselves to God's loving care. Truly there could be no better guide than our faithful God.

Prayer: *Dear Father, thank you for your steadying presence when we lose our rhythm. Help us trust you to guide us each and every day. Amen*

Thought for the day: I can always trust God to guide my steps.

Jessica E. Dutton (Maine, USA)

Not alone

Read Psalm 139:7–12

Even though I walk through the darkest valley, I fear no evil; for you are with me; your rod and your staff – they comfort me.
Psalm 23:4 (NRSV)

Years ago I felt empty and wrapped up in loneliness, and I started walking aimlessly down the road. A passing driver offered me a ride, and we drove to the city of Caguas. I listlessly asked for money on the street so that I could take the bus to San Juan.

I arrived at night and sat near a pier. I thought, 'Life is not worth living,' and walked towards the edge of the water. I noticed a piece of wood on the ground, and when I stopped to pick it up, a pocket-sized New Testament that someone had given me earlier in the day fell out of my shirt pocket. When I picked it up, it was open to Psalm 23. I cried when I read the first verse: 'The Lord is my shepherd, I shall not want.'

I walked for a long time and finally stopped at the Salvation Army centre. The people there welcomed me and offered me a room, toiletries and bed sheets. I stayed for several days and began to experience God's love.

Today, 20 years later, I am secure in the knowledge that Jesus Christ is my Saviour. I am never alone because he walks beside me.

Prayer: *Hear our prayer, merciful God, and fill our hearts with your love. When we feel lonely and empty, lead us from the darkest valley with your saving grace. Amen*

Thought for the day: 'God is our refuge and strength, a very present help in trouble' (Psalm 46:1).

Víctor Lugo Pérez (Puerto Rico)

Expect the best

Read Philippians 4:4–9

More than anything you guard, protect your mind, for life flows from it.
Proverbs 4:23 (CEB)

There's a tunnel just a short distance from my house, and when traffic is light, you can yell out the window of your car and hear a marvellous echo. Whatever you say comes back to you.

That echo is incredibly reminiscent of my life – what I put out there is exactly what I've gotten back. For years I had a negative attitude, filled with doubt, fear and low expectations. I was a firm believer that anything that can go wrong will. And like an echo, I got back exactly what I put out, what I expected and dwelt on.

After my mother passed away, I turned to scripture for comfort. I got an unexpected attitude adjustment. As I took in the stories of God's love, forgiveness, kindness and compassion, my heart changed. I found myself genuinely happy. The more I focus on the goodness of God, the more enjoyable my life becomes. I still have challenges to face, but my heart is lighter as I face them.

Prayer: *Dear Lord, help us to see the world and all who live in it through your eyes. Amen*

Thought for the day: When I focus on God's goodness, I can better see the good around me.

Esther Bonner (California, USA)

Out of the ordinary

Read 2 Kings 5:1–14

Naaman's servants came up to him and spoke to him: 'Our father, if the prophet had told you to do something difficult, wouldn't you have done it? All he said to you was, "Wash and become clean."'
2 Kings 5:13 (CEB)

When Elisha, the man of God, told Naaman what to do to be healed, Naaman initially refused to do it because it seemed so common. He was expecting an extraordinary healing and almost missed a miracle because the road to the miracle seemed unremarkable.

I know there have been times when I have missed out on positive changes because I didn't want to do the ordinary things to make the extraordinary changes possible. I wanted healing in my physical health, but I didn't want to eat less and exercise more. I wanted advancement at work, but I didn't really want to put in the extra time to make myself stand out. I wanted a better relationship with my children, but I didn't want to give up any of my time to make that happen. So many times I've failed to do the things God has called me to do because I was waiting for a miraculous proclamation. I have learned, however, that things won't get better as a result of grand gestures but rather with the dedicated daily efforts of Christians who refuse to give up the faith.

Prayer: *Dear Lord, teach us to do the ordinary things so we can lead the extraordinary lives you have given us. Amen*

Thought for the day: With God's help, ordinary efforts can lead to miraculous outcomes.

Amber Marie Followell (Arkansas, USA)

Take heart

Read Psalm 50:1–15

Call upon me in the day of trouble: I will deliver thee, and thou shalt glorify me.
Psalm 50:15 (KJV)

During the Covid-19 pandemic, many people experienced lockdown and were expected to stay home. This meant that suddenly people had a lot more free time and made choices about how to use it.

From today's quoted verse we know that whatever our situation, God wants us to pray and call upon him. In fact God says that when we do, we will be delivered so that we can give God all the glory and praise. God is so loving and wants to deliver us from our troubles. When we face challenges, we find opportunities for spiritual growth and become more and more dependent on God, realising that without God we are nothing.

So let us be encouraged to repent from our sins and to spend more of our time reading scripture and in prayer.

Prayer: *Heavenly Father, thank you for loving us and keeping us under your protection. Help us to grow closer to you, opening our minds to know your will. And in days of trouble, teach us to live and be like your Son, our Lord, in whose mighty name we pray. Amen*

Thought for the day: I will spend more time with God today.

Anoush Gill (Sindh, Pakistan)

When the music fades

Read John 4:21–24

Therefore, I urge you, brothers and sisters, in view of God's mercy, to offer your bodies as a living sacrifice, holy and pleasing to God – this is your true and proper worship.
Romans 12:1 (NIV)

Several months after Covid-19 emerged in the UK, the church I attend decided to reinstate in-person services. The disease was still prevalent, so many restrictions were in place, which meant we were unable to sing. The first service back felt a bit empty. Having socially distanced seating added to this sense of sparseness, but most of all I noticed the absence of our singing. This did not upset me, but it did challenge my perception of worship.

Often, we hear the time of singing in a church service referred to as 'worship'. Or we feel we need to attend a 'worship service', perhaps to say particular prayers or perform certain actions in a prescribed way, in order for us to have worshipped. Today's reading challenges this assumption. Worship is something profoundly important to our relationship with Jesus and is not limited to just singing songs. In fact, we are told to offer our bodies as a living sacrifice – which is to offer our entire selves. We are called to worship Jesus with all we think, say and do.

So, when the music fades and when we are unable to sing or meet in the same physical space, this does not mean that our worship has stopped. It may just be the thing we need to help us rediscover what worship truly is.

Prayer: *Lord Jesus, show us what it means to truly worship you. Take our whole lives and use them for you glory. Amen*

Thought for the day: Worship is a lifestyle.

Matt McChlery (England, United Kingdom)

Love in action

Read Romans 12:9–21

If it is possible, as far as it depends on you, live at peace with everyone.
Romans 12:18 (NIV)

When I applied for my first job after college graduation, I spent a whole day interviewing with multiple executives. Every interviewer ended by telling me, 'You're a shoo-in for this job.' A month later, the recruiter called to inform me that I was not selected. She relayed to me that all my interviewers thought I wouldn't be able to give a confident pitch to a room full of executives. They said I was too nice and would struggle to navigate the office politics.

It is a misconception that kindness is weakness. Displaying kindness reflects self-restraint. Finding the strength to live at peace with those around us is difficult, but thanks be to God that we can do so by following the blueprint in today's passage of scripture. In some Bible translations, this passage is titled 'Love in action'. Wouldn't it be great if the world displayed more love in action?

As someone whose confidence flows from trust in Jesus Christ, I took it as a compliment to be rejected for this job because I was too nice. Kindness, combined with God's love, can change us and change the world.

Prayer: *Heavenly Father, give us the strength we need to live at peace with everyone. Help us to rejoice in hope, stay patient in affliction and persist in prayer. Amen*

Thought for the day: Today I will display love in action to those I encounter.

Ben Byrum (Texas, USA)

A sparrow's worth

Read Matthew 10:27–31

'Are not two sparrows sold for a penny? Yet not one of them will fall to the ground outside your Father's care.'
Matthew 10:29 (NIV)

As I sat in the garden one summer day watching the birds flit back and forth through a hedge, I remembered this verse. It speaks of how precious we must be if even sparrows are looked after by God. I challenged myself to watch just one sparrow for five minutes.

It was impossible! Not only could I not keep track of the small bird because of how fast it zoomed in and out, back and forth, but they all looked the same to me. Except for the black bib marking on the males, there was nothing to tell any of them apart.

But God knows exactly which sparrow is which; God even has each one of their feathers numbered, just as God knows the number of hairs on our heads. If God watches over every swoop of a sparrow, then the awareness and attention God pays to each of us must be far beyond our understanding.

We can trust our heavenly Father not only with the big things in our lives but the very smallest details too. God is able to see and care about our every tiny worry. Anything that ruffles our feathers, no matter how insignificant the world may claim it to be, matters to God. We can bring any and all of our cares safely to God in prayer.

Prayer: *Dear God, thank you that nothing is beyond your notice. Watch over us and our loved ones just as you do each tiny bird. Amen*

Thought for the day: God sees even the smallest creature with deep awareness and tenderness of heart.

Keren Dibbens-Wyatt (England, United Kingdom)

Going in circles

Read Exodus 13:17–22

When Pharaoh let the people go, God didn't lead them by way of the land of the Philistines, even though that was the shorter route. God thought, If the people have to fight and face war, they will run back to Egypt.
Exodus 13:17 (CEB)

I often become anxious when entering a traffic circle. It is especially challenging when I approach my desired exit but am in the wrong lane. Veering from one lane into the next usually brings a blast of horns from other drivers, so the only option is to stay in my lane and keep driving until I find a way to cross over.

The book of Exodus describes the Hebrew people wandering in the wilderness. When they exited Egypt, God led them along a path that preserved them from threats so they would not return to Egypt and would be prepared to enter the promised land. God did not leave them alone but went ahead of them in a pillar of cloud by day and a pillar of fire by night to show them the way. Going in circles for 40 years until they reached the promised land allowed the Hebrew people to learn to trust God.

Though we may sometimes find ourselves going in circles, we can trust that God has not left us alone but is with us, often in remarkable ways. Prayerful attention to God's presence allows us to exit the circle and find our path to God.

Prayer: *Dear God, we quiet ourselves before you and open our hearts to your Spirit. Help us pay attention to your promptings that say, 'This is the way; walk in it' (Isaiah 30:21). Amen*

Thought for the day: God is with me as I travel my daily path.

Graham N. West (Wisconsin, USA)

True identity

Read 1 John 3:1–3

See what great love the Father has lavished on us, that we should be called children of God! And that is what we are!
1 John 3:1 (NIV)

When I was in college, I could tell which of the many strangers on a bus were fellow students. There was something familiar and similar among those of us who were studying at the same university. Maybe it was the way we dressed or talked or walked. I am not sure what it was, but it was perceptible.

I had a similar experience years later, when I was in another country and in a crowd of people of a different culture and nationality. While walking alone inside a mall, a woman behind me comfortably talked with me in my dialect. Without any introduction, she immediately knew we were from the same country and that we spoke the same language. Something about my Filipino identity was familiar to her.

The same is true with our identity in Jesus Christ. Because of God's love for us, God redeemed us and brought us into relationship with God. Through Christ, we are children of God. When we embrace this identity and live according to Jesus' teachings, others will see our good works and glorify our Father in heaven (see Matthew 5:16).

Prayer: *Heavenly Father, may we always be reminded of your love so we may live out our true identity in Christ. May we honour you all the days of our lives. Amen*

Thought for the day: In Christ, my identity is a beloved child of God.

Lei Cao Garcia-Bote (Kuala Lumpur, Malaysia)

Small group questions

Wednesday 4 May

1 Recall a time when you felt a strong temptation. What did you decide to do? What did you learn from the situation?

2 Do you ever think that it would be easier to simply do something wrong and then ask for forgiveness later? Why might this be appealing? How do you resist this desire?

3 What are some of your strongest convictions? How do they guide your decisions? What does it mean to you to stick to your convictions in your heart?

4 How do you feel knowing that you may fail at something or be ridiculed because of your convictions? Why is it important that you stand firm in your faith, even if that means accepting failure?

5 Who in the Bible besides David stuck firmly to their convictions? What was the outcome of their situation? In what ways are you encouraged by their example?

Wednesday 11 May

1 When you feel joyful, do you want to share your joy with others? Why or why not? Who in your life are you best able to share your joys with?

2 What do you do when your church's sermons are on topics that do not apply to your present situation? Where do you find spiritual guidance when this happens?

3 How does it encourage you to know that God cares about our joys as well as our sorrows? What scripture verses remind you that God cares about our joys? How do you share your joys and sorrows with God?

4 What led you to choose your current church home? If you are looking for a church home, what are you hoping to find in a church? How do you know when you have found the right faith community for you?

5 How do you remain sensitive to the feelings and experiences of others? In what ways do you strive to share in others' joys and sorrows?

Wednesday 18 May

1 What aspects of nature most inspire you? Do you enjoy capturing these experiences in photographs or other forms of art? How does this part of nature reveal to you God's artistry?

2 Do you find it easy to look beyond flaws and focus on the beauty around you? Why or why not? What helps you to focus on the beauty?

3 When is it most challenging for you to look past the flaws in others? Why? How do you think God views the flawed people in your life? How will you try to see what God sees in others?

4 Is it easy or difficult for you to look beyond your own flaws? Why? What do you hope others see in you? In what ways do you attempt to emphasise the good qualities that you want others to see in you?

5 How does your faith community help you to focus on the beauty in your surroundings and in others? How do they focus on the beauty in you?

Wednesday 25 May

1 Do you prefer being self-sufficient instead of having to ask for help? Why? How are the outcomes different when you act alone versus when you ask for help from others?

2 Who has helped you through grief? How did they help you? How do you help others who are experiencing grief?

3   What differences have you observed in your life when others are praying for you? Why do you think the prayers of others have such a perceptible effect?

4   Name some biblical characters and situations that serve as examples of the importance of supporting and being supported by others. How do their actions encourage you to support the people in your life and to accept help?

5   Who in your faith community supports you through prayer, friendship and comfort? How have they changed your life? Why is it important to have someone who supports you?

Wednesday 1 June

1   Where do you go to find peace and rest? Why this location? How does being there change your mindset?

2   Do you ever feel like you need to escape the hustle and bustle? Why or why not? What prayers and spiritual practices help you find calm in such times?

3   In scripture we read that Jesus needed to get away from the crowds and find rest. Why do you think this was necessary? Does it help you relate to him more? Or do you find it hard to understand why Jesus would need time alone with God?

4   How do you breathe in God's peace? Do you find that you are better able to experience God's peace when you are alone or with others? Why?

5   How does your church make time for quiet moments with God? In what ways can you more intentionally seek quiet moments of peace while in community with other Christians?

Wednesday 8 June

1   When obstacles block the way to your goal, how do you usually respond? Do you forge ahead, or do you tend to turn around and abandon your goal? Why?

2 Describe a time when you noticed a parallel between your immediate situation and your larger faith journey. What did you learn that shaped your faith for the future?

3 When you are sad or grieving, do 'briars of sadness' remain for you despite scripture's assurances? What comforts you when you still feel sad after reading scripture?

4 If you have ever recited scripture as you worked, like today's writer, what passage did you recite? What other spiritual practices do you engage in while you work?

5 When and where are you most comforted, refreshed and renewed by God? What is it about that place that helps you feel close to God?

Wednesday 15 June

1 Why do you think we are so quick to value and praise people who work on stage or in the foreground? Why is it so easy to forget about the good work of those in the background?

2 Do you consider yourself a leader in your faith community, or are you most often in the background? Why? Do you consider the work you do important? Why or why not?

3 What forms of appreciation from others mean the most to you? In what ways do you most enjoy showing appreciation to others? Why is it so important to show appreciation for one another's work?

4 Who in scripture comes to mind as someone who worked as a leader, front and centre? Who in scripture served quietly behind the scenes? What do you admire and what can you learn from each of these people?

5 Who in your community is always working in the background? How do they help your community? How might you show them this week that you value their work?

Wednesday 22 June

1 Recall a time when you left something behind. Were you eventually reunited with the lost item, or did you have to leave it behind permanently?

2 Have you ever missed out on something because you failed to ask for it? What kept you from asking? How would you handle the situation differently if you were given a chance to redo it?

3 Do you ever feel that you are undeserving of God's blessings? What makes you feel that way? What scriptures remind you that God wants to bless each of us?

4 When have you confidently asked God for something? Did God give it to you? How might the outcome have been different had you not asked God for it?

5 How do members of your faith community ask for blessings for themselves and others? In what ways does your faith community encourage you to ask God for the things you need?

Wednesday 29 June

1 Today's writer connected what she saw in nature with her faith journey. What have you observed in nature that has taught you about your faith? How has that changed the way you experience God?

2 Do you find it easy or difficult to reveal your vulnerabilities to others? Why? What happens when you share your hurts and heartbreaks with those around you?

3 When someone opens up to you about their 'hollows', how do you respond? What comfort can you offer them? Do you find it easy or difficult to know how to respond?

4 What scripture passages give you the courage to share your heartbreak with others? What prayers comfort you when you are feeling hollow? How does God help you in those times?

5   Why do you think it is important that we share our burdens with others? What difference would it make in your church, your community and the world if everyone openly shared their burdens?

Wednesday 6 July

1   When someone asks how your day is going, how do you respond? Do you keep things formal or allow the conversation to go deeper? How have you been blessed by being asked this question?

2   What locations have provided you with unexpected opportunities to minister to others? How have you allowed God to work through you in these places?

3   When you think of mission opportunities, what comes to mind? How has your understanding of mission opportunities changed throughout your faith journey?

4   Today's writer found a way to minister to others while at work. Do you find ways to minister to others as you go about your day? If so, what are they? If not, how has this meditation encouraged you to do so?

5   What mission opportunities does your church offer? How do you support or participate? In what other ways could your church minister to those in your community?

Wednesday 13 July

1   Recall a time when you had to wait. Did you wait joyfully? Why or why not? How can remaining hopeful and joyful change your experience of waiting?

2   When you realise that something you were hoping for has not yet come to fruition, do you easily become discouraged? What keeps you encouraged and joyful in such times?

3   What scripture verses remind you that your faith is not in vain and that you can rely on God's promises? Why do these verses encourage you?

4   When you are in a season of waiting, what spiritual practices help you to remain confident and hopeful in God? What prayers encourage you?

5   How does your faith community help you to wait joyfully? Why do you think Christian fellowship can make a difference in the way we wait on God?

Wednesday 20 July

1   When you interact with someone you do not like, are you able to look past the tension between yourself and the other person? Do you feel it is important to try to engage such people? Why?

2   How has prayer given you a deeper faith and greater understanding of God's purpose for you? Name the prayer practices that have been the most meaningful to you.

3   Do you find it easy or difficult to pray for someone with whom you have a difficult relationship? Why? How does praying for those who have hurt you change the way you feel about them?

4   Is it easy for you to forgive others? Does God's forgiveness of you change the way you forgive? Why or why not?

5   How are your prayers for others different from your prayers for yourself? In what ways have you sensed the Holy Spirit at work while you pray for others?

Wednesday 27 July

1   Describe a time when a physical reminder of God's presence brought you peace. Why did the reminder help you in that moment? How does it continue to help you?

2   Describe a time when being assured of God's presence helped you when you were feeling anxious or sad. Why was God's presence particularly comforting during that time?

3   What are the most important physical reminders for you of God's love and presence? How do you remember God's presence in the absence of these physical reminders?

4   When have you felt distant from God? What made you feel this way? What brought you close to the creator again?

5   What stories in the Bible about God's constant presence encourage you the most? How do you keep these stories in mind when you are feeling anxious or alone? In what ways do these stories strengthen your faith?

Wednesday 3 August

1   How do you respond when faced with a life change that doesn't seem exciting to you? When is it easiest for you to fall into patterns of complaining and dread? How do you avoid getting stuck in such patterns?

2   When you aren't happy about a situation, do you still give thanks to the Lord? Why or why not? In what ways does giving thanks change your mindset?

3   What practices best help you to turn your mind and heart towards gratitude? How do you remind yourself of what God has done for you and all that you have to be thankful for?

4   Who in scripture do you think best demonstrates gratitude? Who do you know that models gratitude well? What can you learn from them?

5   How does your faith community talk about gratitude? Is giving thanks an act of prayer, a monetary gift, a way of living? Or is it something else? How do you show others and God that you are grateful?

Wednesday 10 August

1 Today's writer learned more about his faith through his experience of lifting weights. What experience in your life has taught you about your faith? Describe what you learned.

2 Recall a time when you were frustrated by a period of transition, only to see in hindsight that the transition was important. How has that experience helped you face other times of transition?

3 How are you encouraged to know that our struggles can strengthen and prepare us for things to come? What else brings you peace and confidence in times of struggle?

4 What stories from scripture feature people whose faith was strengthened through change and adversity? How do you use times of transition to draw closer to God?

5 How does your community encourage your faith when you are experiencing change? How do they help you grow wiser, stronger and closer to God?

Wednesday 17 August

1 Has your life or the life of a loved one ever been dramatically changed due to an injury or illness? How did your community respond? Name some ways you or your loved one received love and care.

2 How do you care for others who are in difficult circumstances? What do you find most challenging about caring for others? What is most rewarding?

3 When has your life been blessed by the care of others? When has someone offered you help without having to ask for it? In what ways has this affected how you care for others?

4 How are you encouraged by biblical examples of communities that cared for their members? Which of these examples is the most meaningful to you? Why?

5 Who in your community needs care right now? How will you care for them? How might you continue to care for them beyond their immediate situation?

Wednesday 24 August

1 Where is your favourite place to hear an echo? Before reading today's meditation, had you ever thought of an echo as a parallel to your life? Why or why not?

2 When have you gotten back what you put out into the world? What did this teach you about your attitude and the way that it can affect your perspective?

3 How does scripture help you in times of grief or sorrow? Where else do you find comfort?

4 What prayers, spiritual practices or scripture passages help you to focus on God's goodness? Why do you think focusing on God's goodness helps you to see the goodness around you?

5 Who in your life consistently puts out goodness into the world? How do their actions bless others and themselves? What do you most admire about this person? What can you learn from them?

Wednesday 31 August

1 When have you been part of an easily identifiable group? What made the group identifiable? Describe that experience.

2 When you are in an unfamiliar space, how do you feel when you find someone you can connect with? Why do you think finding common ground with others is so encouraging?

3 What does it mean to you to be a child of God? How do you embrace that identity? In what ways might others be able to perceive this identity in you?

4 Today's writer describes several of her identities — a university student, a Filipino woman, a child of God. What are your identities? As you live into your other identities, how do you allow your identity as a Christian to shine through?

5 How do you find common ground and community with people who are different from you? In what ways does Christian faith bond people and give them a shared identity?

Journal page

Become a Friend of BRF
and give regularly
to support our ministry

We help people of all ages to grow in faith

We encourage and support individual Christians and churches as they serve and resource the changing spiritual needs of communities today.

Through **Anna Chaplaincy**
we're enabling churches to provide
spiritual care to older people

Through **Living Faith**
we're nurturing faith and resourcing
life-long discipleship

Through **Messy Church**
we're helping churches to reach out
to families

Through **Parenting for Faith**
we're supporting parents as they raise
their children in the Christian faith

Our ministry is only possible because of the generous support of individuals, churches, trusts and gifts in wills.

As we look to the future and make plans, **regular donations make a huge difference** in ensuring we can both start and finish projects well.

By becoming a Friend of BRF and giving regularly to our ministry you are partnering with us in the gospel and helping change lives.

How your gift makes a difference

£2 a month — Helps us to develop **Living Faith** resources to use in care homes and communities

£10 a month — Helps us to support churches running the **Parenting for Faith** course and stand alongside parents

£5 a month — Helps us to support **Messy Church** volunteers and resource and grow the wider network

£20 a month — Helps us to resource **Anna Chaplaincy** and improve spiritual care for older people

 ## How to become a Friend of BRF

Set up a Direct Debit donation at **brf.org.uk/donate** or find out how to set up a Standing Order at **brf.org.uk/friends**

Contact the fundraising team

Email: **giving@brf.org.uk**
Tel: +44 (0)1235 462305
Post: Fundraising team, BRF, 15 The Chambers, Vineyard, Abingdon OX14 3FE

Good to know

If you have any questions, or if you want to change your regular donation or stop giving in the future, do get in touch.

Registered with

FUNDRAISING **REGULATOR**

SHARING OUR VISION – MAKING A ONE-OFF GIFT

I would like to make a donation to support BRF.
Please use my gift for:

☐ Where it is most needed ☐ Anna Chaplaincy ☐ Living Faith

☐ Messy Church ☐ Parenting for Faith

Title	First name/initials	Surname

Address

	Postcode

Email

Telephone

Signature	Date

Our ministry is only possible because of the generous support of individuals, churches, trusts and gifts in wills.

giftaid it You can add an extra 25p to every £1 you give.

Please treat as Gift Aid donations all qualifying gifts of money made

☐ today, ☐ in the past four years, ☐ and in the future.

I am a UK taxpayer and understand that if I pay less Income Tax and/or Capital Gains Tax in the current tax year than the amount of Gift Aid claimed on all my donations, it is my responsibility to pay any difference.

☐ My donation does not qualify for Gift Aid.

Please notify BRF if you want to cancel this Gift Aid declaration, change your name or home address, or no longer pay sufficient tax on your income and/or capital gains.

Please complete other side of form

SHARING OUR VISION – MAKING A ONE-OFF GIFT

Please accept my gift of:

☐ £2 ☐ £5 ☐ £10 ☐ £20 Other £ [_____]

by (*delete as appropriate*):

☐ Cheque/Charity Voucher payable to 'BRF'

☐ MasterCard/Visa/Debit card/Charity card

Name on card

Card no. [_] [_] [_] [_] [_] [_] [_] [_] [_] [_] [_] [_] [_] [_] [_] [_]

Expires end [M][M] [Y][Y]   Security code [_][_][_]   Last 3 digits on the reverse of the card

Signature   Date

☐ I would like to leave a gift to BRF in my will.
Please send me further information.

For help or advice regarding making a gift, please contact our fundraising team +44 (0)1235 462305

Your privacy

We will use your personal data to process this transaction. From time to time we may send you information about the work of BRF that we think may be of interest to you. Our privacy policy is available at **brf.org.uk/privacy**. Please contact us if you wish to discuss your mailing preferences.

Registered with

FUNDRAISING **REGULATOR**

 Please complete other side of form

Please return this form to 'Freepost BRF'
No other address information or stamp is needed

BRF

Bible Reading Fellowship is a charity (233280) and company limited by guarantee (301324), registered in England and Wales

UR0222

Grief Notes
Walking through loss
The first year after bereavement
Tony Horsfall

In *Grief Notes* Tony Horsfall charts the first year of his grief journey since the death of his wife from cancer. Month by month he tells the unfolding story of walking with and through loss, weaving this together with biblical teaching on grief and insights gained from grief counselling. With a poignant mix of honesty and humour, Tony shares the challenges of rebuilding his life and reflects on how he has seen God meet his needs as he wrestled with grieving in a time of lockdown and pandemic.

Grief Notes: Walking through loss
The first year after bereavement
Tony Horsfall
978 1 80039 126 0 £8.99
brfonline.org.uk

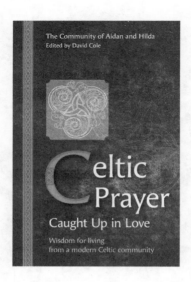

Even the most committed pray-ers can get stuck in a rut. Loved and familiar ways of praying can become dry and stale and it can be difficult to rekindle the spark, especially if you've only ever known a handful of ways to pray. But help is at hand in this wide-ranging and exciting new collection from the Community of Aidan and Hilda. Accessible and inspiring, it will refresh your spirit and draw you deeper into knowing God.

Celtic Prayer: Caught up in love
Wisdom for living from a modern Celtic community
The Community of Aidan and Hilda, edited by David Cole
978 1 80039 053 9 £12.99
brfonline.org.uk

How to encourage Bible reading in your church

BRF has been helping individuals connect with the Bible for 100 years. We want to support churches as they seek to encourage church members into regular Bible reading.

Order a Bible reading resources pack

This pack is designed to give your church the tools to publicise our Bible reading notes. It includes:

- Sample Bible reading notes for your congregation to try.
- Publicity resources, including a poster.
- A church magazine feature about Bible reading notes.

The pack is free, but we welcome a £5 donation to cover the cost of postage. If you require a pack to be sent outside the UK or require a specific number of sample Bible reading notes, please contact us for postage costs. For more information about what the current pack contains, go to **brfonline.org.uk/pages/bible-reading-resources-pack**.

How to order and find out more

- Email **enquiries@brf.org.uk**
- Telephone BRF on +44 (0)1865 319700 Mon–Fri 9.30–17.00
- Write to us at BRF, 15 The Chambers, Vineyard, Abingdon OX14 3FE

Keep informed about our latest initiatives

We are continuing to develop resources to help churches encourage people into regular Bible reading, wherever they are on their journey. Join our email list at **brfonline.org.uk/signup** to stay informed about the latest initiatives that your church could benefit from.

Subscriptions

The Upper Room is published in January, May and September.

Individual subscriptions
The subscription rate for orders for 4 or fewer copies includes postage and packing:

The Upper Room annual individual subscription   £18.30

Group subscriptions
Orders for 5 copies or more, sent to ONE address, are post free:
The Upper Room annual group subscription   £14.55

Please do not send payment with order for a group subscription. We will send an invoice with your first order.

Please note that the annual billing period for group subscriptions runs from 1 May to 30 April.

Copies of the notes may also be obtained from Christian bookshops.

Single copies of *The Upper Room* cost £4.85.

Prices valid until 30 April 2023.

Giant print version
The Upper Room is available in giant print for the visually impaired, from:

Torch Trust for the Blind
Torch House
Torch Way
Northampton Road
Market Harborough   Tel: +44 (0)1858 438260
LE16 9HL   **torchtrust.org**

**All our Bible reading notes can be ordered online by visiting
brfonline.org.uk/subscriptions**

☐ I would like to take out a subscription myself (complete your name
and address details once)

☐ I would like to give a gift subscription (please provide both names
and addresses)

Title .... First name/initials .... Surname ....

Address ....

.... Postcode ....

Telephone .... Email ....

Gift subscription name ....

Gift subscription address ....

.... Postcode ....

Gift message (20 words max. or include your own gift card):

....

....

Please send *The Upper Room* beginning with the September 2022 /
January 2023 / May 2023 issue (*delete as appropriate*):

Annual individual subscription ☐ £18.30

Optional donation* to support the work of BRF £ ....

Total enclosed £ .... (cheques should be made payable to 'BRF')

*Please complete and return the Gift Aid declaration on page 159 to make your
 donation even more valuable to us.

Method of payment

Please charge my MasterCard / Visa with £ ....

Card no. ☐☐☐☐ ☐☐☐☐ ☐☐☐☐ ☐☐☐☐

Expires end ☐☐ M M ☐☐ Y Y   Security code ☐☐☐   Last 3 digits on the
reverse of the card

All our Bible reading notes can be ordered online by visiting brfonline.org.uk/subscriptions

☐ Please send me .... copies of *The Upper Room* September 2022 / January 2023 / May 2023 issue (*delete as appropriate*)

Title .... First name/initials .... Surname ....

Address ....

.... Postcode ....

Telephone .... Email ....

Please do not send payment with this order. We will send an invoice with your first order.

Christian bookshops: All good Christian bookshops stock BRF publications. For your nearest stockist, please contact BRF.

Telephone: The BRF office is open Mon–Fri 9.30–17.00. To place your order, telephone +44 (0)1865 319700.

Online: brfonline.org.uk/group-subscriptions

☐ Please send me a Bible reading resources pack to encourage Bible reading in my church

Please return this form with the appropriate payment to:
BRF, 15 The Chambers, Vineyard, Abingdon OX14 3FE

For terms and cancellation information, please visit **brfonline.org.uk/terms**.

Bible Reading Fellowship is a charity (233280) and company limited by guarantee (301324), registered in England and Wales

To order

Online: **brfonline.org.uk**

Telephone: +44 (0)1865 319700 Mon–Fri 9.30–17.00

Delivery times within the UK are normally 15 working days. Prices are correct at the time of going to press but may change without prior notice.

Title	Price	Qty	Total
Grief Notes: Walking through loss	£8.99		
Celtic Prayer: Caught up in love	£12.99		

POSTAGE AND PACKING CHARGES			
Order value	UK	Europe	Rest of world
Under £7.00	£2.00		
£7.00–£29.99	£3.00	Available on request	Available on request
£30.00 and over	FREE		

Total value of books	
Postage and packing	
Donation*	
Total for this order	

* Please complete the Gift Aid declaration below

Please complete in BLOCK CAPITALS

Title .... First name/initials .... Surname...

Address ....

.... Postcode ....

Acc. No. .... Telephone ....

Email ....

Gift Aid Declaration

giftaid it

Please treat as Gift Aid donations all qualifying gifts of money made

☐ today, ☐ in the past four years, ☐ and in the future **or** ☐ My donation does not qualify for Gift Aid.

I am a UK taxpayer and understand that if I pay less Income Tax and/or Capital Gains Tax in the current tax year than the amount of Gift Aid claimed on all my donations, it is my responsibility to pay any difference.

Please notify BRF if you want to cancel this declaration, change your name or home address, or no longer pay sufficient tax on your income and/or capital gains.

Method of payment

☐ Cheque (made payable to BRF) ☐ MasterCard / Visa

Card no. ☐☐☐☐ ☐☐☐☐ ☐☐☐☐ ☐☐☐☐

Expires end ☐☐ ☐☐ Security code ☐☐☐ Last 3 digits on the reverse of the card

Please return this form to:

BRF, 15 The Chambers, Vineyard, Abingdon OX14 3FE | **enquiries@brf.org.uk**

For terms and cancellation information, please visit **brfonline.org.uk/terms**.

Bible Reading Fellowship is a charity (233280) and company limited by guarantee (301324), registered in England and Wales

Enabling all ages to grow in faith

Anna Chaplaincy
Living Faith
Messy Church
Parenting for Faith

100 years of BRF

2022 is BRF's 100th anniversary! Look out for details of our special new centenary resources, a beautiful centenary rose and an online thanksgiving service that we hope you'll attend. This centenary year we're focusing on sharing the story of BRF, the story of the Bible – and we hope you'll share your stories of faith with us too.

Find out more at **brf.org.uk/centenary**.

To find out more about our work, visit
brf.org.uk

Sharing *the* Story *since* 1922